CW00693347

WHAT DO YOU DO WITH YOUR TIME?

Sunday Adelaja

WHAT DO YOU DO WITH
YOUR TIME?
©2017

ISBN 978-966-1592-63-5

London, United Kingdom
sundayadelajablog.com

You can take a hold of your life situation when you answer the question, What Do You Do With Your Time. My aim with this book is that so, you can define your time, see where it is currently going, and get a vision of what is possible for you to achieve with it.

Cover Design by Olexandr Bondaruk

WHAT DO YOU DO WITH
YOUR TIME?
London, United Kingdom
All rights reserved.

TABLE OF CONTENTS

PREFACE

Looking back at my life, it is almost inconceivable that there was a time when I used to be in a dilemma as to what to do with my time. It is with awe I now consider that millions of people are still in a similar situation. What a burden, pain and tragedy that is for grown up people to wake up in the morning and not know what to do with their time.

Friends, there are many frustrations in life, different types of dilemmas, all sorts of disillusionments. I however think that the most frustrating of all this is having legs and feet yet wake up in the morning and not know what to do with yourself. I am sure I will not be exaggerating if I say millions if not billions of people are experiencing this feelings of pain, frustration and disillusionment. Is there any solution for them? Is there any way out?

Thank God the answer is here at last. This book - What to do with your time will deal a deadly blow to this plague. If as a result of this some people will get direction in their lives to come out of the hopelessness of not knowing what to do with their time, I will consider my 50 years in life as fulfilling. Please spread the word. There is an answer, there is a solution to the question of what to do with your time.

For the Love of God, Church and Nation.

Dr. Sunday Adelaja.

INTRODUCTION

Og Mandino, the best-selling American au... and speaker, wrote his famous 10 scrolls on success and wisdom in the book, The Greatest Secret in The World. He had, at one time in his life, contemplated suicide after being plagued by alcoholism and depression. A very poignant scroll he penned is Scroll Number 5. Here is an extract:

I will live this day as if it is my last.

This day is all I have and these hours are now my eternity. I greet this sunrise with cries of joy as a prisoner who is reprieved from death. I lift mine arms with thanks for this priceless gift of a new day. So too, I will beat upon my heart with gratitude as I consider all who greeted yesterday's sunrise who are no longer with the living today...

I will live this day as if it is my last.

I have but one life and life is naught but a measurement of time. When I waste one I destroy the other. If I waste today I destroy the last page of my life. Therefore, each hour of this day will I cherish for it can never return. It cannot be banked today to be withdrawn on the morrow, for who can trap the wind? Each minute of this day will I grasp with both hands and fondle with love for its value is beyond price. What dying man can purchase another breath though he willingly gives all his gold? What price dare I place on the hours ahead? I will make them priceless!

I will live this day as if it is my last.

I will avoid with fury the killers of time. Procrastination I will destroy with action; doubt I will bury under faith; fear I will dismember with confidence. Where there are idle mouths I will listen not; where there are idle hands I will linger not; where there are idle bodies I will visit not. Henceforth I know that to court idleness is to steal food, clothing, and warmth from those I love. I am not a thief. I am a man of love and today is my last chance to prove my love and my greatness.

Og Mandino was acutely aware of the importance of time in life's equation that he had to dedicate a whole chapter in his signature work to emphasise how critical it is. The question that this book, "What Do You Do With Your Time", seeks to answer pertain to getting you the reader to see how important these precious seconds are that we all seem to let pass.

I believe one of the biggest dilemmas of adult life is the question, What Do You Do With Your Time? Have you ever truly asked yourself this? As children growing up, it was never necessary to ask because our time was planned for us by others. Parents, teachers and adults generally scheduled our life activities. So, it was simple. I go where my mother tells me to. I do what my headmaster tells me to. When my father tells me to get into the car, I obey.

The real question only comes when we grow up and there is no one there to direct us. We now must make up our minds and decide what to do with our time. Many of

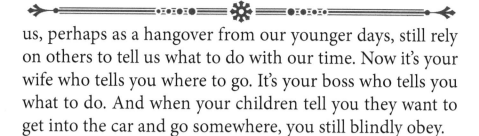

us, perhaps as a hangover from our younger days, still rely on others to tell us what to do with our time. Now it's your wife who tells you where to go. It's your boss who tells you what to do. And when your children tell you they want to get into the car and go somewhere, you still blindly obey.

Are you sleepwalking through your life, never realising the decisions that you have abdicated to others about time? The early church leader, Paul of Tarsus, challenged his readers in one of his letters to the first European churches, to stop acting like children,

"When I was a child, I talked like a child, I thought like a child, I reasoned like a child. When I became a man, I put childish ways behind me."

1 Corinthians 13:11

You are a grown woman or man. You must grow out of the childish tendency to let others answer the question of what you do with your time. Most of us are moving like zombies through life and the result is millions of accumulated hours that are being wasted around the world. There are books that are unwritten, cures to diseases that are going undiscovered, inventions that are not coming to fruition. All because we cannot account for what we are doing with our time.

When we are ignorant of our time and its value, then we end up doing things that kill time instead and we get cheated out of time by those who understand it more. The entertainment industry thrives because of people's need to kill time. The world system is strong because it cheats workers to spend their time working it for cheap compensation. It is truly a sad state of affairs.

It doesn't have to be this way, however. You can take a hold of your life situation when you answer the question, What Do You Do With Your Time. My aim with this book is that so, you can define your time, see where it is currently going, and get a vision of what is possible for you to achieve with it.

I believe that if we get a hold of this truth and put it into practice, like what I am doing, we can change our nations, our governments, our national economies and our churches.

CHAPTER 1
LIVING ON
PURPOSE

CHAPTER 1
LIVING ON PURPOSE

To start everything off, I would like to present the premise to you that understanding your purpose is the crucial first step that makes you see the relevance of even asking this question in the first place. If you don't think you have a purpose on earth, then you will not see your time as valuable. Instead it is just free time to be used on basic things. Let us see how purpose ignites you.

THE POWER OF PURPOSE

When you read the book "Dreams From My Father" by former president of the United States Barack Obama you will see a man who understood that he was going to do something significant in his life. Having been elected as the first African American editor of the Harvard Law Review, the young Obama did not know exactly where he would end up in life, but he knew something special was in his future. He was approached to write his memoirs in the book "Dreams From My Father" and proceeded to expose the thinking that shaped the man who would open doors for black people all over the world.

In that book, Barry (as he was known at the time) talks candidly about how he felt growing up with white grandparents and a white mother. He shows the way that he experienced the horrors of war in Indonesia where he lived during his mother's marriage to his stepfather. He also talks about finding out about his father's family in Kenya. It is almost scary to think of the kind of foresight he had to articulate these kinds of things before he even held public office. However, this is an example of a man who knew his life had a purpose.

You too can have this kind of purpose in your life. When you have goals for your life and when you have purpose for your own life, then you will know what to do with your time. Purpose will give you the reason to count your days with a sense of urgency. You will understand and know that you do not have as much time as you think to achieve all that you are meant to. If you knew you were going be an influential government leader, what would you be doing with your time? Would you be asking other people? Would you give responsibility for your development into the man or woman you need to be to your boss? Or would you find a way to get it done yourself as quickly as possible?

Jamie was a very intelligent telecommunications engineer. He was a senior operations engineer working for the biggest phone provider in New Zealand. An avid explorer, you would be almost certain to find Jamie tinkering around with the computer system looking for more efficient and easier ways his team could do their job.

Jamie only had one ambition and that was to become a Shift Manager. He had worked 15 years at the same company and it looked like he was in line for the next opening for promotion. He did everything he was told by his bosses to do to prepare for the position once an opening came up, but fear of rocking the boat of his financial security prevented him from looking outside the company for other opportunities to do things he loved.

When a shift manager finally retired and interviews were held for the position, Jamie thought he was due to finally get that job he wanted. Unfortunately, the newly appointed Service Delivery Manager of the company decided he wanted to bring in an external applicant and Jamie did not get the job. He has to wait at least another ten years for the next retirement.

Jamie put his career and purpose in the hands of the management team he worked for and they did not decide in his favour when it counted. You do not want to have this kind of scenario to happen to you, do you? So, you must take the decision of what to do with your time into your own hands.

The question of this book is What Do You Do With Your Time? Without a purpose to why you exist, you will be stuck in the situation I described in the introduction where you abdicate the responsibility of answering this question to other people. Abdicating is when a king refuses to take on the duties of a ruler and the throne passes to whoever is

next in line. This is what you are doing when you get other people to decide how the time of your life is spent. You are a king, but you have let the privilege to rule in life to be given to another person. This is a sad situation to be in.

This book is a continuation from the book, "Why Losing Your Job Is The Best Thing That Could Happen To You". This is where I first explored the idea of the importance of the free time you have when you are not working. You can search for this book on Amazon or Ocada books if you are in Africa. The question "What Do You Do With Your Time" follows on perfectly from these ideas.

WHERE DOES YOUR FREE TIME GO?

What do you do with your time when you are unemployed? This question is extremely important to the young and old of our countries because the unemployment numbers are so high. In Nigeria, around 26 million men and women were unemployed or underemployed in 2016. In the United Kingdom, 1.64 million people were out of paid employment and in the United States, 7.8 million people were unemployed in 2016.

What do you do with your time after you have been fired? What do you do with your time after you lose your job? With the world economy, as uncertain as it is these days, a lot of people are finding themselves without a job through no fault of their own. Retrenchment and redundancies

are happening a little too often for comfort and many of you are concerned that you could be a victim.

You do not need to have lost your job for the question to apply to you. What do you do with your time when you're alone? When work has finished and you sit down after your day's labour. Where do you go in that precious little moment? What do you do with your time when there's nothing to do? At the weekend? In the evenings? What do you do with your time when you have all day to do nothing? You have a lot of time that needs accounting for. This is your challenge.

An example of this type of behavior is Queen. She is a Nigerian lady living in Canada. A rail engineer by trade, she has the life she dreamt of growing up. Her husband and three children, together with her job, keep her quite busy. After work, Queen and her husband help their children with any work they have from school, then they sit down for a bottle of wine after dinner.

From nine o'clock in the evening until midnight they watch the best shows on the television, the favorites being Scandal and Empire. Without fail, their routine is set for them. Both feel that it helps them to de-stress from their tightly wound work and life schedule.

The life that this couple lives is typical of many seemingly successful couples around the world. How many hours do they spend on television though? Fifteen to twenty

per week? Sixty per month? How much does this really add up to? How much do you spend in your evenings? What if these hours where put to better use to build their dreams and better their lives?

You too can be busy like Queen and her husband going around in circles that you have no time for real progress. This is the reason that I'm presenting the question to you. What Do You Do With Your Time? If you are not careful the time can pass without you having slowed down long enough to even take stock and try and be purposeful about your life.

I believe that this question crosses all our minds at some point. What we do with time may differ on how purposeful you are as a person. But everyone must know how to live out this question and audit their life so that they can answer. The answer may not be what we want to hear but it is worth answering. It may well be the same as lifting a rock in your garden. You may not like the bugs that you see at first but now that light and illumination has entered that area you will be able to move forward.

I truly believe that for every person sitting in the pews of your church, they have also asked themselves the question, What Do You Do With Your Time? If anyone has not then they are totally walking in darkness in maximising their life and they need to ask it right away. When you do this, you will be able to know what to do going forward.

BEING PRODUCTIVE

The reason I say we should have at some point asked ourselves this question is because I think everyone must be able to make their time productive. I submit that you must do something of worth with your time.

"Amateurs sit and wait for inspiration, the rest of us just get up and go to work."

Stephen King, Best-selling author

Having sold over 350 million copies of his books, Stephen King knows all about getting on and getting to work. As an author of fiction and supernatural books, he would know a thing or two about using free time well. I use his words to challenge you to be productive on purpose.

The whole book is going to be exploring this premise of being productive. It is a measure of our success as people - being industrious. In the following chapters, we will discuss what someone who lives on purpose and with goals should be doing with their time.

We will look at the way that productivity should be measured when we use the standards of the Kingdom of God. This will be looking at time itself and the acceptable way that I suggest you measure it. Included in that we will be looking at are the different things you could be doing with your time and you will decide which one is best for you.

As a purposeful person, even your time spent in church is going to be challenged and examined. Be prepared.

In this first chapter, we looked at the importance of how knowing your purpose or calling is important to your life. If you believe you have something worthwhile to achieve besides the mundane things of everyday living, then you will be shrewder about how you spend your time. You will not be too eager to let it pass by. In the next chapter, we will look at how time is measured as a starting point for showing how to make the most of it.

THE GOLDEN NUGGETS

1. When your life has goals and purpose, you will know what to do with your time.

2. What do you do with your free time? When you can answer this question in the right way, you are going to have a productive life.

3. Everyone in the world needs to know how to answer for themselves the question, What do you do with your time?

4. When everyone is able to make their time productive, our nations and the world will become better.

CHAPTER 2
MEASURED TIME

CHAPTER 2 – MEASURED TIME

In chapter 1, we saw that the person who is living a life of purpose is aware and deliberate about what he or she does with time. I do not think you would be reading this book if you were not such a person of purpose. You would not be using your time to learn the concepts of using time wisely in this book. In this chapter, we will see that time must be converted and to do that, the first thing you must understand how to measure time.

TIME MUST BE CONVERTED

"This is the key to time management - to see the value of every moment."

Menachem Mendel Schneerson,
20th Century Jewish Rabbi

Widely considered as one of the most influential Jewish leaders of the last century who built schools, drug rehabilitation centers and synagogues, Menachem Schneerson is someone who certainly saw the value of time. It is important to realize that your own time must be converted and I will show you why and how.

The general principle that I want you to remember going forward is that time must be converted. It is so important we will need to repeat it. Time MUST be converted. Conversion is defined as the act of changing or causing something to change from one form to another. This must be what you do with your time. You need to convert it into something that is of value and that is tangible.

Everything that we discuss comes out of this rule. How you convert your time is up to you and your particular calling but even the smallest measurement of time that you possess needs to be converted. You can convert it to knowledge, wisdom, relationships, money, virtue or strength. In fact, you can convert time into any product you want.

Michael Jordan scored more than 32,000 points over the course of his stellar basketball career, and earned six NBA championships. He is, by acclamation, the greatest basketball player to ever grace the court. Many fans of the game remember his spectacular 72-win season but few ever talk of his days as a 5'10» high school player without a dunk.

In 1978, Michael Jordan was just another boy in the gym, along with 50 or so of his classmates, trying out for the Emsley A. Laney High School varsity basketball team. This was the first team for his school. There were 15 roster spots. Jordan—then a 15-year-old who was only 5'10» and could not yet dunk a basketball—did not get a spot. The team needed height and he was embarrassed not to have been selected. He went home, locked himself in his room and cried.

Then he picked himself up and turned the cut into motivation. "Whenever I was working out and got tired and figured I ought to stop, I'd close my eyes and see that list in the locker room without my name on it," Jordan would explain. "That usually got me going again." Jordan, using that sizable chip on his shoulder to his advantage, spent the next year as the star of the junior varsity team. He put up multiple 40-point games and attracted crowds that were unprecedented for a JV affair.

The summer after that, Jordan began to grow. In 1979, he grew 4 inches and worked out constantly. That year he made the varsity squad and instantly became Laney High's best player, averaging more than 20 points a game. Despite having secured his spot on the team, Jordan's work ethic didn't drop off. In his final year, he led Laney High to a 19-4 win-loss record. Jordan capped off his high school career in style, being named an All-American. He was not yet the man who would later be called His Airness, but he was well on his way!

Instead of waiting a year to be picked, Michael Jordan saw that he had a year that he could be converting to turn himself into the best basketball player his school had ever seen. This concept of converting time is powerful because it has the potential to change your life. You too can use time, like Michael Jordan, to make yourself into the best version of yourself. What do you want to become? You must now begin to convert time to become world class at that thing.

TO MEASURE TIME

You do not have as much time as you think! Time is measured normally as seconds, minutes, hours, days, weeks, months and years. Many of us who are older have actually started measuring time in terms of the decades we have seen. This is a recipe to wasting time if I am to be honest with you.

If you want to be aware of time more acutely, and I challenge you to do this, you need to be more deliberate with how you measure your time. The very maximum allowance you should give when measuring and assessing your time is a day package. This has been something I have done and it has made me extremely efficient. I understand that if you had been previously thinking in terms of the years, months and weeks you live, then it will be a shock to your system to do what I'm suggesting. However, keep reading this book because you are going to see the arguments I will put forth to convince you this is the better way to be a good steward or manager of your time.

Rick and Rex are identical twins who have a completely different approach to this concept. They do not measure time in the same way, so Rick spends all his free time in the pub with his friends while Rex is always working on his football blog.

Rex started writing about his favourite football team Chelsea FC 10 years ago. At that time, they were studying

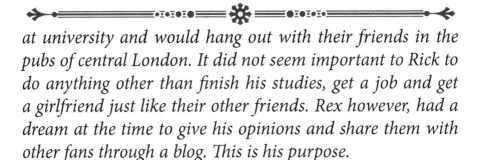

at university and would hang out with their friends in the pubs of central London. It did not seem important to Rick to do anything other than finish his studies, get a job and get a girlfriend just like their other friends. Rex however, had a dream at the time to give his opinions and share them with other fans through a blog. This is his purpose.

Rick never noticed the time going past but Rex put all his spare time going to matches, travelling with the team, creating relationships with some of the staff as well as other super fans of Chelsea. A day would not pass by that he did not write something, record some video or otherwise work on his blog.

The contrasting results are plain to see between these 2 men. At 30, Rick is going nowhere and stuck in the same routines with the same people as 10 years ago. Rex, on the other hand, has become the biggest blogger in the Chelsea football club fandom. The club invites him to go to their events, advertisers pay him to run adverts on his website and he makes three times as much as he would have working in the field he studied. He brings joy and entertainment to many people around the world.

Time has got to be measured in a manner that shows that we understand the urgency of the situation. Which of these brothers has the type of life that you would rather enjoy? The one living his destiny or the one who is throwing time into the trash? You have to decide.

A lot of people experience the feeling of time flying past. If you have ever had a job, imagine the last time you had a week off work. At the start, you think you have all the time in the world, however, it feels like the time is over before you can even blink an eye. Before you know it, that familiar feeling of dread comes over you as the last day of your week off draws to a close. Weeks pass this quickly, months pass this quickly, and ultimately, years also pass like water in a flowing river.

Time must be measured in seconds, minutes and hours. The day is the largest unit of time that you must use when you evaluate what you do with your time. You do not have a week. You do not have a month. You definitely do not have a year!

So teach us to number our days that we may get a heart of wisdom.

Psalm 90:12

The Psalms were ancient meditative songs written by Israelite kings, priests and prophets. The one quoted above eludes to what I am saying. When you number your days, that is when you count properly the time you have left in your life, you will develop an attitude that God considers to be wise and prudent.

Each of these packages of time need to be converted. It is not good enough to be allowing time to pass without getting anything tangible at the end. Like Michael Jordan who refused to let his year go past and have him risk not being selected for the team yet again the following year, you must take your life into your own hands and convert time. Hours must be converted.

Seconds and minutes must be converted. Hours must be converted. Days must be converted.

CONVERTING A DAY

I said earlier that you must work with a day at a time. This is the premise to real productivity that I am going to put forward in this book. What I consider to be truly knowing what to do with time, is to convert one day properly. This is the answer to the question What Do You Do With Your Time? You must convert a day. This is the logical conclusion if I ask you What Do You Do With Your Time? And the principle we are working with on that is we must convert our time. Then you have to convert a day.

And to convert a day is to produce a product. Each day of your life needs to be measured by the product that results from it. This is how you know that you are doing something of value with your time.

«Are you a good time manager?» This is the other way to ask our titular question. The way you assess yourself in answering this is by the product that you have coming out of that particular day. God will ask you this question at the end. In fact, He is asking it to you right now through this book.

Can we ask this question of a country? What answer would we get? What does Ghana do with its time? What does Nigeria do with its time? What does Japan do with its time? Collectively as a nation, what does the USA do with its time? When the rulers of a nation ask themselves this question, starting from those at the top all the way to the person on the lowest rung of society, this will answer national questions that are concerning the population. When everyone, or at least the majority of people, in the country is making it a habit to convert their days well, then the economy will improve. The literacy rate will improve when teachers and students ask themselves the question what do we do with our time?

Take the nation of Japan as an example. As a nation, Japan has been deliberate about being productive. Consequently, the people really take productivity seriously. The Prime Minister, Shinzo Abe, and his administration consider boosting the productivity of their private sector as part of their job. A community of productivity bloggers and writers are emerging who are starting to help raise the lagging cultures of the 90s to move into the 21st century. They test newest technologies and apps and approach their productivity and efficiency very thoroughly.

If you think about it, most of the brands we know in high-tech (and cars) come from Japan (Sony, Fujitsu, Nikon, Panasonic… Toyota, Nissan, Mazda…). It is all thanks to their working ethics… and the way they diligently learn new things. The country is intentionally trying to help their people translate this productivity into the current information age. It can only be helpful to the people and the nation as a whole.

Are you a good time investor? Investing time is something that we will take a closer and more in-depth look at in the soon to come chapters. We have to measure our effectiveness by converting that particular hour, that particular minute, that particular second. The is what I mean by converting the day.

BEING EFFECTIVE WITH TIME

One day an expert in time management was speaking to a group of business students and, to drive home a point, used an illustration those students will never forget.

As he stood in front of the group of high powered overachievers he said, «Okay, time for a quiz".

Then he pulled out a one-gallon, wide-mouthed jar and set it on the table in front of him. Then he produced about a dozen fist-sized rocks and carefully placed them, one at a time, into the jar. When the jar was filled to the top and no more rocks would fit inside, he asked, «Is this jar full?»

Everyone in the class said, «Yes.»

Then he said, «Really?» He reached under the table and pulled out a bucket of gravel. Then he dumped some gravel in and shook the jar causing pieces of gravel to work themselves down into the space between the big rocks.

Then he asked the group once more, «Is the jar full?»

By this time, the class was on to him. «Probably not,» one of them answered. «Good!» he replied. He reached under the table and brought out a bucket of sand. He started dumping the sand in the jar and it went into all of the spaces left between the rocks and the gravel. Once more he asked the question, «Is this jar full??»

«No!» the class shouted. Once again he said, «Good.» Then he grabbed a pitcher of water and began to pour it in until the jar was filled to the brim.

In this illustration, the objects being placed inside the jar represent what constitutes your available time of life. It is rich with possibility! The big rocks represent the days that are in your life. The gravel represents hours and sand represents minutes. The water then represents your seconds. What do you do with your days, your hours, your minutes and your seconds? There is much intentional activity you can fit in if you are intentional and deliberate about it.

Time comes in seconds, minutes, hours, days, so to be productive you need to be operating in the habit of converting all these. To live a life of understanding and wisdom is to not waste time.

To conclude, we have seen in this chapter that time needs to be broken down into its units of measurement. When scrutinised in this way, then it is easier to see that time is passing you by and you can now assess how effective you are in using it. Now ask yourself, am I using my time well? In the next chapter, we will define what wise time investment is.

THE GOLDEN NUGGETS

1. To know what to do with time, is to convert one day properly.

2. Time must be converted into product.

3. How do you measure time? The day should be the biggest unit you use to measure time. Anything bigger is unacceptable if you intend to use time wisely.

4. Convert each day, hour, minute and second for maximum efficiency.

5. You must learn how to convert a day. To convert a day is to produce a product.

6. To assess how good a time investor you are, look at the product you have produced with the time you have.

7. To live a life of understanding is to not waste time.

CHAPTER 3
INVESTING TIME
WISELY

CHAPTER 3 – INVESTING TIME WISELY

In this chapter, we are going to follow on the last chapter's focus which was how you must measure your time appropriately in order to understand how to use it wisely. Now we will see exactly how you could be using your time, followed by the wisest use of time – investing it.

"Lost time is never found again."

Benjamin Franklin

Even Benjamin Franklin, the influential father of the American Enlightenment of the 18th century, understood how crucial it was to treasure time. Take this words to heart as you go through the lessons and principles in this chapter.

WASTING TIME, SPENDING TIME AND INVESTING TIME

You have three options of what to do with your time; you can waste it, spend it or invest it. In the book, "How Losing Your Job Is The Best Thing That Could Happen To You", I explored fully what these three things look like in real life but allow me to go over the basics again. It is very important. You can waste, spend or invest time, but to be truly effective in your life, you must invest your time.

Mary, Helen and Barbara are sisters. They grew up together in the same house but now, as adults, they live totally different lives. Mary has a husband who takes care of her, so she does not do much with her time. She wakes up in time to kiss her husband as he goes out the door. After that she sits and watches morning television while eating breakfast. At midday, she takes a walk out to the park where she spends an hour or two with the dog. On her way back, Mary passes by the shop to pick up some food. She then watches YouTube videos and goes on social media until she has to get food ready for her husband. Mary wastes a lot of her day.

Helen is single and hard working. She lives an exciting life as a hospitality manager in charge of air hostesses for a major airline. When Helen flies, she is responsible for everyone on the plane, both hostesses and passengers. Only the captain outranks her on the plane. This is a busy life. She lives between London and Singapore for most of the year. Extremely well paid, Helen has a lifestyle to show her status. High class shopping and an elegant apartment are the least she could have in return. She never seems to have time at the end of the day. Helen spends her time.

Barbara is the youngest sister of the three. Married by a shrewd man, she has learnt to value their time. Her husband helped her to see that she has a great teaching gift. He happens to be a musician highly sought after by high end hotels. When Barbara had her two sons she decided that her time would be best used in teaching herself how to homeschool them. Now that they are of school going age, she has taken *on their education as her full-time career. She also has three other children of wealthy friends who she teaches. The extra income this gives them allows Barbara and her husband to invest in their future. They invest their time.*

Now what is the difference, between engaging in these three activities? When you waste or spend time, it has passed and gone without much to show for it. However, when you invest your time you are multiplying it and reproducing yourself in the process.

Time is multiplied when you engage in activities that multiply the value that you get from money. Instead of the straight exchange of time for money that you get when you go to a job, you get a multiplied value back for your time in the form of employees who make money for you, residual and increased income from a business or even products you own that give you a legacy like books you have written. Reproducing yourself is when the result of what you have done with your time is that other people can get the value of what you produce.

Mary the time waster is in the worst predicament. When she wastes time, she does not even get compensated for it at all. She gets nothing in return for the hours she spent walking around town and talking to her friends on the phone. Most days when asked about her day by her husband, she struggles to recall what she did! She is truly just throwing time in the garbage. It is so sad.

Now Helen at least remembers what she did with her time. She goes to work on a daily basis on long haul flights and she can at least point to the pay package she gets as some sort of compensation. Like Esau in the bible who sold his birth right for a plate of stew, so is Helen. She is selling out her birth right a little each day, but at least she gets some little stew for it.

Modern day slavery however, is not in chains, it is in debt. By being in debt in the form of credit cards to keep up her lifestyle, she has locked herself to always need work. It was actually better when she had a lower paying job. Now she is in real financial trouble.

TIME IS LIFE

Imagine a jar filled with water. The jar serves as a picture of your life. Your body is represented by the jar and the water inside is your life. It is not the jar that is your life. That is the outer container. When you go to work each day, it is as if you are pouring some of that water into a cup. A certain amount is gone, you have sold it to your employer but at least you got some cash in return.

This time spent phenomenon is not only happening with work. The same happens when you go to school to get your run of the mill education. It happens as well when you go to church religiously. It may have some value culturally and you will remember what you did (unlike wasted time) but this is time you will never get back.

Let me show you how spent time can just slip away. You may remember getting married. You have the photos and the video to reminisce over it. Perhaps you remember having your kids. I hope you remember having your children! You may be able to point out that you have been a Christian for ten years and you have been in church for all this time. This is spending time. Yes, you remember doing these things, but there are no tangible fruits to your labour. For the purposes of what we are doing with this book I am not counting simply having children as tangible fruits to your labour. Animals have babies simply by existing so it is not a higher-level activity.

When you waste time, you do not remember what it was that happened to it. When you spend it the only thing you have to show is that you have grown old. Perhaps have some children running around. This is not the kind of tangible results I am trying to bring out in this book. However, your children are separate people in God's eyes, with their own lives to live. One day your children will move out of your house and start their own families and you will be left to wonder what you did with all your days.

This is what is happening when the members of our churches experience «empty-nest» syndrome later in their lives. If our churches want to help couples to avoid marital issues in their mid-lives you must teach them not to only live their lives for their children. They will regret it later.

IT IS BEST TO INVEST TIME

This alternative is much better. When time is invested, you do not lose it. Instead you are multiplying it by converting it into a better form either in other people or in a product. A life lived in this way is the kind of beautiful life I want to teach you how to live. Let me show you what to do with your time. If the people in a nation are taught this and how to live this way, they will be much more productive so as to lift up the economy of a nation.

It is equally vital that you are aware of what you need to invest in and how long it should take to yield a product.

Tudor Bismark, leader of the Council of African Apostles, once said, «*Your world is a reflection of your wisdom.*» If you are not living a fulfilling and exciting life, you have not been actively considering learning how to invest your time. This particular bit of wisdom is not in you yet and that is okay. You can learn it now!

As we conclude, we pointed out in the last chapter that life is measured in time. It is measured in hours, minutes and seconds. It therefore follows that to waste or lose time is to waste or lose life. When you are simply living your mundane life, and walking around in the world like most of the world population. If all you do is sleep and wake up, drink, eat and gossip on the phone, you are wasting precious time.

And here is what you are doing when you are spending time. By going to work on a daily basis you may feel you have done something special with your time. You may even believe that because of your high salary you are better than the lower paid unskilled workers. Though you may be getting paid the time is still going with each passing second. You will never see it again. That is just the way life is. It will never come back.

There is only one problem with spending time. The problem with this is that you are not multiplying the time entrusted to you. Time given is such an incredible resource that is too important to sell off to the highest bidder. All you have engaged in is a straight exchange of money for time and this is not enough. It is not the wisest decision you can make on using your time. You are not multiplying the Kingdom of God as you have been mandated to. It is not the highest use of your time.

In the coming chapter, we are going to see what true time consciousness looks like. I challenge you to ask yourself this question, «When I have free time, what do I do so that it is not wasted or spent?» When I ask, What Do You Do With Your Time, this is the way I want you to think. I want you to interrogate yourself as to what your free time looks like first of all. Are there any holes in your day that you cannot account for? This, of course, is wasted time. Are there any activities that you can do that can invest this time?

What Do You Do With Your Time? What do you do with your time so that it is well invested? Take time out right now to write the answer to this question. It will change the way you look at your life and your time. There is too much at stake to let seconds and minutes pass by. These are the very seconds and minutes that will turn into hours and days. As hours and days pass on, so does your whole life. One day you are young and eager and before you know it you have passed into the territory of the old.

THE GOLDEN NUGGETS

1. There are three ways to use your time; wasting, spending or investing it. To be effective you must invest time.

2. Time wasted or spent is time gone. Multiply yourself by investing time.

3. Wasting time is the same and throwing time away in the garbage.

4. Time spent may be remembered but it is simply an exchange. You are selling your birth right.

5. Time invested is not lost, it is multiplied instead.

CHAPTER 4
TRUE TIME
CONSCIOUSNESS

CHAPTER 4
TRUE TIME CONSCIOUSNESS

Last chapter, we saw how important it is to avoid wasting time and even spending it on seemingly acceptable activities like work or church. It is much better to invest our time wisely. In this chapter, we will unravel the value of time and see some examples of how to be truly time conscious.

THE VALUE OF TIME

"Until you value yourself, you will not value your time. Until you value your time, you will not do anything with it".

M. Scott Peck,
Author of The Road Less Travelled

The author here, a psychiatrist who served as an administrator in the US government, is trying to show that when you have no real understanding of what time really is, you will not use it well. This is the whole premise of what I have been saying. What then, is the value that you have placed on your time?

As we continue from the last chapter we recognise that we must understand the value of time. For you not to waste time, you must first begin to look at time correctly. This will also help you to not fall into the trap of just spending your time. M. Scott Peck's quote above shows us that the value we hold of our time is tied up in how we value our own lives and ourselves. If we place a small value on our lives and our time, then it follows that it will be difficult to do anything worthwhile with time like investing it.

Value has been defined as the worth of something in terms of the amount of other things for which it can be exchanged. This means that when you are looking to assign a value to your time on earth you have to compare the amount of other things that can be exchanged for it. What can you exchange the day that you are living right now for? Of the amount of «things» that are in your life, is there anything that can compare in value to your time? What would you want to get in exchange?

Let's say I offered you a book for one day of your life. Would that be enough? Perhaps that one is a bit of a no-brainer. What if I offered you a pair of shoes? Would they be worth it? How about the amount of gold that would be equivalent to a day in your life? Would a small coin be worth it? Or a slightly bigger gold nugget? How about a pile of gold coins? A little closer to home though, how much money would you take in exchange for a day in the one life God gave you? Would it be $10? Or $100? Or $1000? This is the value you are putting to your time for a day of work.

ASSESS YOUR TIME IN DAYS

In order to be able to put time into the correct perspective, I recommend that the maximum package you use to assess it be a day. This is my personal recommendation. You can see time in terms of seconds, minutes and hours but the maximum has to be a day. You cannot look at time as weeks, months, years or longer. These units are too large for the concepts that I am attempting to lay before you.

You lose your urgency when you begin to think in weeks or months. Efficiency becomes very difficult to attain at this macro level. Go down to the micro levels instead and the smaller the unit you hold yourself accountable to, the better. Being able to know what you do with each hour is better than measuring each day and knowing each minute is even better.

Consider Stephen and Michelle, two writers who write the same kind of books but work very differently. Both are part-time writers who write in their free time, however they consider their time in differing ways.

For Stephen, free time is any time he has when he is not at work. Because of this, he stays up late after so that he can put in four hours of writing, five days a week. When he writes a book, therefore, it takes him one to two months between coming up with the concept and coming up with his finished product.

Michelle only works with a whole week when she writes. She is unable to see the worth of a few hours here and there to write. For her "process" to work, she must have undisturbed stretches of time. So, Michelle only writes when she has a full week off work. The result of all these starts and stops is that Michelle takes two or three years before she has a book ready.

What is the difference between these two writers? The way they value their time causes them to be productive in very different ways. The time Michelle takes to produce one product, Stephen will have multiple products. Which one of these two are you more like in your approach to time? To be regarded as truly time conscious, you must be like Stephen. Your results will also be similar.

This is where conversion comes into the equation. To maximise life and time you ensure that every hour of the day that comes is converted into some value. You must make sure every minute is converted into some product. Every second has to converted into some investment. Time has to be changed or turned into something of value and the value needs to be something that you see as being commensurate value.

FREDERICK MCKINLEY JONES:
A CASE STUDY

Frederick McKinley Jones was an African American inventor born in 1893. This man is known for his inventions and innovations that changed the transportation of perishable goods. He is the first African American to be elected into the American Society of Refrigeration Engineers.

When you consider that Jones had over 5 dozen patents to his name, it seems like as if he was an extraordinary man. As a young mechanic, he taught himself electronics to the point where he constructed a transmitter for his town's radio station. Much of his scientific and manufacturing prowess did not appear to come from formal education. To the contrary, he had left school at the age of 11 to start work as a cleaning boy. How did he get to be this well versed in mechanical engineering, his niche field of expertise?

From the age of 14, Frederick McKinley Jones worked as a mechanical engineer in Cincinnati, Ohio. He had however, already started building on his ability and inventive mind with self-education and independent study. When he was a boy, instead of concentrating on the misfortune of being a black boy with no parents, he decided to spend his days and nights with his books, tools and in the workshop. Even as poverty and discrimination threatened to stifle his attitude, he had a one-track mind about him as he knew what he wanted to do with his life.

Today, Frederick Jones is a recipient of the US National Medal of Technology. He understood the value of time to bring out the best in him every time he got down to do what he did best. Have you found where best you can maximise your time? Are you conscious of the time you are letting slip when you do not get going at this thing? This is what will give you value that is better than money.

Many of us live life as if we are just «there». What I mean by this is that we seem to be floating in and out of our existence. The biggest sign of this is if you ever feel as if your days are blurred together into one giant unclear mass. Do you ever wonder whether it was Tuesday or Wednesday that just passed you by? This is what I am talking about.

This is not the responsible way to live your life. You must live a life where you are self-conscious all the time. At all times, there must be definite purpose to you actions and your time spent. Are you living conscious of the right now? You need to be living this moment as fully as possible because you will never see it again. Consider the following:

Frederik Eklund is considered by many to be one of the most successful real estate brokers in the city of New York. He is the star of the Bravo reality television show Million Dollar Listing New York which highlights the thrilling world of buying some the most luxurious and expensive property on the planet.

Born in Sweden, Frederik dreamed of going to the United States for a career in sales. He had always been good at that and at the age of 10 had fallen in love with the city of New York. In the time before he moved to America permanently, Frederik used his years to sharpen his selling skills and his personality, which produce a large part of his selling success. The results have been incredible.

Frederik Eklund has closed over $5 billion in residential real estate deals! He is a Managing Director of his own company and leads the top selling team at Prudential Douglas Elliman – the largest real estate brokerage on the US East Coast. Frederik has been the broker to the rich and famous and has the lifestyle to go with it.

If you ask him, he will tell you that all he is doing is maximizing the opportunity he has in his favorite city to make his dreams comes true. At all times, he is creating relationships, entertaining potential clients and researching his market.

The principle that I am bringing out is that you have to be conscious of the time and how you use it to be the best at your craft. If the workers in the real estate in your country thought like this, they would lift the market to world class standard to rival, New York, London and Dubai. So, start waking up to the time you have today.

QUESTIONS TO ASK YOURSELF

Consider these very important questions with each passing minute. Right now, am I wasting life? Right now, am I spending life? Right now, am I converting life? The first two questions cannot be answered yes, all the time if you hope to live the life of success. The prevailing answer for the champion should be no to the first two and yes to the last question. No to wasting your life and no you cannot be stuck in activities that are solely spending your time. Yes, you should be converting your life into things, products that are of value both to yourself and to others. You get to a life converted only by being faithful with the small act of converting a second, converting a minute and converting an hour. Your day needs to be converted. This is what you should be doing with your time.

Let me give you a powerful exercise that will be a worthwhile habit to buried into your life. Make a habit of stopping in the middle of your day and asking yourself, «What am I doing right now?» If you ask it at strategic parts of your day you be inadvertently doing an audit of your time and what you do with it. Whether you are wasting, spending or investing it at any particular moment. The bulk of your productive days needs to be spent investing time by converting it. If this is not the case and you are mostly spending time at work or simply wasting it then change is needed with haste. Converting is the only value adding activity of these three options and will bring your life to a level of effectiveness that God requires.

What is the consequences of what I am doing now? When you stop and consciously ask yourself this, you are finding out how what you are doing affects your life and those of the ones you love. Perhaps you are wasting time. What is the consequence of this, that you are causing your spouse to feel like they are the only one carrying the load of the relationship? Is the consequence the same as you taking food from the mouths of your children? If you are spending time, the unintended result is your deteriorating health as you get older and your body ages with the load of your job. Is the result of your worrying about money and you having a short temper with your wife?

Now let's imagine you are converting your life. The effect of converting time into wisdom could be that you are latter acknowledged as an expert in your field that you can name your price for your services. The effect of converting your time into value in the lives of some protégés of yours could be that one of them later surpasses you and becomes the President of Nigeria. At this point she invites you into her inner circle of advisors and together you work to change the nation. The consequences of what you do daily need to be seriously considered.

A moment of time has the potential to make you better. In a given moment you should ask yourself this question, "What is the value I am adding to myself?" The hour you have is like a seed, and the first and best thing you can do with the seed of time is to add value to yourself. It is practically impossible to do all the other incredible things

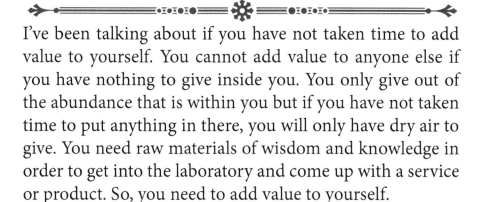

I've been talking about if you have not taken time to add value to yourself. You cannot add value to anyone else if you have nothing to give inside you. You only give out of the abundance that is within you but if you have not taken time to put anything in there, you will only have dry air to give. You need raw materials of wisdom and knowledge in order to get into the laboratory and come up with a service or product. So, you need to add value to yourself.

Then you can move onto the next question. Am I adding value to others? With your time have you looked at who you can invest time into? The best way to multiply yourself and what God has placed inside you is to go and invest in other people. Teachers do this with students. There is a reason you remember certain teachers, lecturers and mentors. They imparted part of them into you and you go with that wherever you go. Who have you added value to today?

Your time needs product as an end result. What is the product that this is going to give me? Is there even a product that the activity you are doing is producing? If not then why not? If more companies asked these questions of their employees there would be a lot less inefficiencies in our economies. In management language, there is something called «sideways energy». For the purposes of our book I'll define it as when teams within an organisation decide to do work that is not in their lane. If everyone in the team asked, «What is the product that this is going to give me?» There would be an alignment very quickly as we realised that

what we are doing is simply spending time. Bureaucracy is the enemy of success in our industries.

Let me give you another way to ask the question. What are the services I'm producing? In the service and knowledge economy of the 21st century, many products that you can produce are in the form of services as opposed to physical goods. Could you come up with a way to help your pastor? Could you devise something that can help a company, a CEO, the government? This could be something you can package in a way that can be monetised. Or are you being a time waster in that moment when you ask yourself the question? Are you too busy with activities like church, that mean you can't devise these services? Then you are losing time.

Lastly as I ask you What Do You Do With Your Time, we come right round to the initial question you need to be asking yourself. Am I investing in myself?

To summarise, we have been looking at length at what it means to be really time conscious. You have to know the value of each and every single day that you live. Do you know this? If you do not, you will end up thinking time is just flying by without your knowing. You must avoid this at all costs. You are better than that and I challenge you to ask yourself the questions, that help you know exactly what your time is accomplishing. Next chapter I will be taking on these questions in a sector of our society that means a lot to me as a pastor – the Church.

THE GOLDEN NUGGETS

1. Start looking at time correctly if you do not want to waste or simply spend it. To do this you have to assess each second and minute the right way.

2. Every day must be converted into a product, value or investment.

3. Live a self-conscious life, constantly checking what you are doing with the time.

4. Are you adding value to others? Are you investing in yourself?

CHAPTER 5
TAKING ON
CHURCH
TRADITION

CHAPTER 5
TAKING ON CHURCH TRADITION

In the last chapter, we looked at some questions you should ask yourself about what you do with your time. In this chapter I want to dig a bit deeper with some of those questions but focusing my questions as well as directing my challenge to the churchgoing readers.

FOR CHURCH GOING CHRISTIANS

«Does anyone have the foggiest idea of what sort of power we so blithely invoke? Or, as I suspect, does no one believe a word of it? The churches are children playing on the floor with their chemistry sets, mixing up a batch of TNT to kill a Sunday morning. It is madness to wear ladies' straw hats and velvet hats to church; we should all be wearing crash helmets. Ushers should issue life preservers and signal flares; they should lash us to our pews.»

Annie Dillard,
Pulitzer winning author

The author of the quote above, Annie Dillard, presents a challenge to people of faith and likens the power of belief to explosives. If you claim to be a Christian, do you know the power of what you practise? Christians who do not understand how to harness this power are like children at play. I am going to show you how this applies to you if you are using your time in an unwise manner.

The question should be asked with every passing minute, «Why am I here? Is my being here giving me any product?» I believe for Christians it is extremely important that this also be asked when you are in church as well.

Some Christians, like Stan from Nigeria, spend a lot of time attending church. He attends Monday and Tuesday morning prayers which are each two-hour long. On Wednesday, there is a fellowship meeting of the street evangelism group he belongs to, then he goes to evening service. Thursday is the small group meeting at his home. Fridays, he spends at the all-night prayer meeting. Then on Saturday there is usually a social occasion like a church picnic, followed by three services on Sunday!

This may seem extreme but many readers who have been brought up in an African church environment will be laughing to themselves because they know someone or people spending extraordinary amount of time in churches. This is definitely not a wise way to spend time for Christians. When those who we are trying to help, who are not Christians, but understand a bit about how time should be spent, see this they are repelled to us and our message. Your church would probably attract more high quality members if it avoided this kind of fanaticism among its members.

FOR THE SAKE OF TRADITION

The behaviour I am describing above is especially prevalent behaviour among Africans and people from my own country, Nigeria. Going to church seems to be a fashion trend in itself. It is unfortunate that some of us just go to church like dummies. There does not appear to be any rational reasoning behind our fanatical church attendance. I am a pastor of a very large church myself, so you must understand that me saying this is not getting me any fans but I have to say it.

This is how I speak as someone who professes to represent God. In the natural, if I was seeking my own intentions, I would tell you to go to church more, perhaps even encourage you to change churches to mine. However, I have no intention of that whatsoever. I have my own church which is big enough. A lot of you are going to church every day and every week without fail. Just because it is tradition.

Here is what Jesus had to say about tradition. It is important to hear what the founder had to say:

«And so, you cancel the word of God in order to hand down your own tradition. And this is only one example among many others."

Mark 7:13 NLT

From this passage, it is plain to see that tradition for the sake of tradition was not something Jesus advocated. There was a lot of traditional practices among the Jews that he lived amongst in his day. Tradition for its own sake is not necessarily a good thing. Jesus basically said, «Because of your tradition you have made the power of God of no effect.» Tradition, according the Master, is one of the only things that can make God's power null and void. Think about that the next time your prayers and petitions appear to be going unanswered. Jesus, the God of the universe, expressly says to us, «If you want to see My power brought to nothing, then carry on with your pedantic acts of piety."

What is tradition? It is a long-established or inherited way of thinking or acting. Traditions are those things that you just do emotionally because this was the way that your fathers and mothers always did them. Those things you do instinctively. You almost do not even need to think about doing them, they just get done automatically. The actor Woody Allen, stated that, "Tradition is the illusion of Permanence." And in so argues that our traditions give us security hence traditions are things you do customarily. They have turned into customs. Take those customs and rituals that your ancestors used to practice back in their day, for example. You may think of them as silly superstitions now but if you removed yourself from your emotional attachment to your own church attendance, you would recognise that now you have your own traditions.

An instance of culture is the belief among Asians living in the United Kingdom (who came from India and Pakistan typically) that their children must go to universities when they are of age. In the past, Asian immigrants needed to do this because university degrees in sectors like accounting and medicine ensured they had better jobs than their parents.

Today, parents in this community are sending their children to university regardless of whether the children want to or not. Kid who do not know what they want to do with their lives are being coerced to put themselves into debt and commit to three and four year courses just for the social standing of their parents in the community. There are many cultural norms that mould our actions.

There is a danger to these types of traditional thinking. You begin to think thoughts like, «This is what the whole country does. This is what my culture does. This is what all good Christians do.» The second you start to think this way you are no longer thinking for yourself. You are allowing a culture to decide the way you live for you and it is so easy to get carried away by these strong traditions and beliefs. Before you know it, you are doing something that was never meant to be done by someone in your particular set of circumstances.

For most of us, our natural lazy mind loves this! To not have to think for yourself but depend on the way it has always been done. It becomes easy, then, to blame our

circumstances on our culture and say, «Well, I cannot do anything to change things for myself.»

THE PHARISEES: TRADITIONALIST TO THE CORE

It is interesting to look at the Pharisees, who always seemed to be so enamoured to their religious that they clashed with Jesus many times. Who are the Pharisees, you may ask? This sect came out of the deportation and exile of many Jews from Judah to Babylon by the king who conquered them, Nebuchadnezzar. The fall of Jerusalem and the destruction of Solomon's temple led to many changes in Jewish culture and religion. During the 70-year exile in Babylon that is recorded in the biblical books of Daniel and Ezekiel, houses of assembly and houses of prayer started cropping up in the absence of a central Jewish temple and a line of priests. Various schools of teachers rose out of these ashes of disarray to become sects that all taught different things.

When Nehemiah led a lot of the exiles back to rebuild Jerusalem, the need arose to have a central vein of teaching in the newly built temple. The Pharisees came out of this time period. They were given the backing of the common people and enjoyed positions of prominence in public life. Being sticklers to their understanding of the law of Moses, they consistently challenged Jesus about matters relating to the law and their traditions. The Pharisees, as do many leaders in churches today, had a knack for portraying

their own rules as if it was the word of God Himself. Jesus constantly destroyed these fictitious rules.

THE MYTH OF SUNDAY

Which brings us nicely to the myth that Sunday is the holy day of God on which you must go to church. What do you do with your time when it comes to Sunday and general church attendance? Christians have for centuries argued that Sunday and Saturday (whichever one your particular church sees as the Sabbath) is the holy day of the Lord and you must be in church without fail on this day. Have you ever given deliberate thought to why you are in church every single Sunday? I can hear some of you already saying, «But this is God, Pastor Sunday. This is God's day!» Before you stone me, consider the following argument I am putting forth.

Have you ever asked yourself, «Is going to church the best way I could invest in myself today?» Even when it comes to going to church. I know it may be a stretch to you. Maybe you have spent your whole life believing in going to church religiously, even if there is nothing to show for it. The questions I presented to you in the last chapter still apply. When you go to church, are you wasting time, spending time or investing time in yourself? Do you even remember what was spoken at your church last Sunday? If not your time has been wasted. If you remember but the message is not something that you are converting then you are just spending time. To be investing in yourself you must

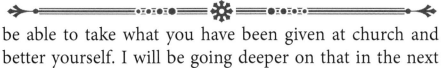
be able to take what you have been given at church and better yourself. I will be going deeper on that in the next chapter.

AFRICAN CHRISTIANS: A CASE STUDY

Allow me to churn your way of thinking a little. Could you use that time? Could you have used those hours for something more productive? For some of us reading this book, I am talking about four or five hours on a Sunday and a whole night prayer session on a Friday. Half of the people in all-night prayers are asleep anyway and they have found ways of looking like they are praying silently. All they want is to check the attendance roster to impress the church leader or pastor. The amount of African people who are simply mumbling incantations they memorised while they are in a half-dead stupor. All this so that we can show badges of honour to other church members or so we are not looked down at by our fellow Pharisees! This is true foolishness for the sake of tradition.

This is not what Christians should be doing with their time. While we do all this, we are mistaken that these are the things that please God. Acts of religion are not what pleases God. He sees what is happening inside your heart, not just what you do outwardly. We are thinking, «Well this is God! We must go to church.» It has been drummed into our heads continuously that church attendance is the one thing. Among Nigerians, there is a type of Christianity I will call cultural Christianity. It is all over Africa as

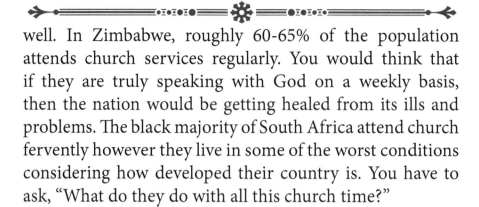

well. In Zimbabwe, roughly 60-65% of the population attends church services regularly. You would think that if they are truly speaking with God on a weekly basis, then the nation would be getting healed from its ills and problems. The black majority of South Africa attend church fervently however they live in some of the worst conditions considering how developed their country is. You have to ask, "What do they do with all this church time?"

Is going to church the only way you can serve God? Are you sure there are no other alternatives? I want you to think outside the church-created box for a while. This will change your life and it will change the lives of the people who are in your church. Consider the millions of people who attend church in Nigeria. If only one tenth of the combined hours they spend in church on a Sunday was redirected and spent doing the things that God actually called them to do, there would be so many testimonies of the wonderful things evident in their lives.

Here is something that is going to shock you. In going to church you are not actually serving God. Going to God's house (church) is not your act of service to Him. You are supposed to go to God to invest in yourself. I have a series of messages that I recorded on Prayer and one of the premises that I explored in that series is that prayer is somewhere you go to get a revelation of God and of yourself. Visit my YouTube channel (search «Sunday Adelaja official») in order to go through these messages as they will be very useful to you.

But back to church attendance, when you go to church and enter the presence of the Lord, you are investing in yourself. In His presence, you will see Him more clearly and fellowship with His Spirit. This in turn will enrich YOU. As you spend more time with Him, He brings out things in you that He hid at your creation and He shows you how you can become a better man or woman. This is what you are supposed to go to church for. Not as an act of service, thinking that somehow by lifting your hands in a worship song you are adding to God and that will make Him pleased with you.

There are two reasons you go to church. When we go to church the purpose should be to either add value to ourselves, or to add value to others. This is how the maturing believer should see church attendance. It is immature and deceptive when we teach God's people that they are serving God by coming religiously to church. Perhaps a bit manipulative as well. So, do not be deceived or guilted by tradition to attend church blindly.

Perry attended a two-year course that her church was running. It was a weekly course that ran for three hours every Monday evening. The course was meant to take someone from being a young believer with little knowledge of faith or the bible to becoming a leader in life.

The first year of the course was all about learning the foundations of Christian faith and then applying them to one's life. Perry learnt how to pray, how to understand what she read in the bible and what wisdom was. All these things were put to practice and she felt like she could live her life with more purpose with these teachings.

In the second year, she was introduced to the concept of being a leader in life once she realized she was a Christian. How to work, be a good wife and how to raise children in a way that glorified God were some of the things taught in the course. At the end, Perry came out of the experience as a more valuable member of society who represented God better.

This is an example of what I recommend is a worthwhile use of your time at church. This is the kind of church activity that is beneficial to you.

At church, you should either add value to yourself or to others. This is how it should be. Unfortunately, this is not the case in most situation. This is not why most people go to church and it is sad. People are not being taught right. You are supposed to be going to be taught something that will raise your level of producing. To be honest though, most times we already know everything that is being said at church because we have been there so many times already, maybe since we were children. Hence, we are not adding value to ourselves. We just go there to feel good through attendance.

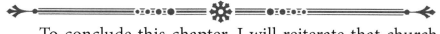

To conclude this chapter, I will reiterate that church tradition is not enough for people who want to be effective in life. Going to church alone out of tradition is discouraged by Jesus Himself. It does not gain you points of approval with God. Instead, you must attend church to become better and to help other people. Let me show you in the next chapter what it could look like instead!

THE GOLDEN NUGGETS

1. When attending church activities, ask yourself, "Why am I here? Is my being here giving me any product?"

2. Do not attend church like a dummy just because it is tradition.

3. Jesus challenged traditions because they nullified God's power.

4. Do not be ruled by culture and societal pressure to attend church blindly.

5. The act of church attendance is not service to God. You go to church to add value either to yourself or others.

CHAPTER 6
WHAT COULD YOU
DO WITH YOUR
TIME INSTEAD?

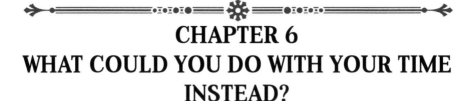

CHAPTER 6
WHAT COULD YOU DO WITH YOUR TIME INSTEAD?

I spent the last chapter showing you how a lot of what we do at church with regular attendance is wasting or at best spending time. There is not much investing of that time happening. In this chapter I will show you an alternate reality. These will be practical options that, if implemented, would be a help to our nations. Whether it be in Ukraine or the USA, United Kingdom or Nigeria, Japan or Argentina, if we carry out these solutions we will change the fortunes of the populations of our countries.

"Baseball is like church. Many attend few understand."

Leo Durocher,
Hall of fame baseball player and manager

Even though baseball legend Leo Durocher said these words in jest, there is an element of truth to the fact that many Christians do not understand what church is truly for. Let me challenge your perceptions in this chapter.

SAVE AND INVEST CHURCH TIME

Let us say instead of religiously going to church throughout the week, you saved then invested those three or four hours? Maybe on the weekdays you did something else with your time. Do you really need to be at all those night watch prayer meetings? You could go to church only once or twice a week.

How about taking that time and using it to bring more glory to God?

A lot of time is invested in the church with the notion that an individual's success is determined by their time spent in church attendance. There is no direct notion to support this school of thought. However, we are of the premise that if you back up that time spent with actively working towards the solution to your circumstances. Then you are onto becoming a winner. For example, if you are facing financial challenges, yes one should pray over the matter. But it has to be backed up with action of applying to work, registering with agencies or attending courses. In essence whatever it will take for you to move to a higher level.

This is done when the actions that you carry out are of such benefit to humanity that they cannot help but attribute it to your faith. When you multiply, yourself you are expanding your Creator's Kingdom on the earth and He is the One Who gets all the glory or praise. Glory to God is not

only in a song you sing with your hands raised up in church on a Sunday. Real glory comes when tangible territory is taken for the sake of Christianity in the name of Jesus Christ.

Songs are good, but actual victories in battles you are fighting for God are something that lacks in modern day Christians. Consider God as your King and you are His soldier. When you go ahead and do your duty as a soldier fighting for Him, He is pleased. Being able to carry out your purpose is pleasing to God. This is better option for things you can be doing with your time.

Let me give you an example. If Ola, a medical research scientist, stays home on a particular Sunday and does his research on finding a cure to cancer, it is a good thing. Maybe he goes to the library to read up on some very important information that he has not been able to read during the week. If Ola works on his project or goes to the laboratory, he would be able to get somewhere in what he is doing.

He works on some weekends instead of going to church in the traditional manner. Now all this time Ola is working on his personal relationship with God on his own. He grows in God, loving Him, and has fellowship with his family and friends. I believe this is an acceptable course of action for him to take, despite how the more religious members of his church may look at him.

Ola is similar to you in many ways. You too have a purpose that you must be working on; a land of your own that you must be tending to. You need to appropriate some of your church time to do your work in your garden. It will be time better spent than at the church that does not add to that.

BRINGING MORE GLORY TO GOD

I guess that right now every religious bone in your body is screaming in protest at what I am suggesting, but please bear with me and allow me to expand on my thesis. The uncomfortable truth is that time that is spent solving a problem on the earth will bring more renown, or glory, to God than years of going to church with nothing to show for it. Examine the years that you have been going to church. What have you been producing and what tangible evidence do you have to show for it? If there is nothing, then you are deceiving yourself if you think attending church is your service to God.

Let us get back to our friend Ola who we used as an example in the last section. He should, by all means, go to church in the times when it works out for him but if he has to work on his God-given purpose, he should. There are a lot of people who try to make people feel guilty when they do not go to church. Pastors, elders, other members and family members look at you funny when you have not been to church. People in the UK, for instance, would feel at ease getting out of church to catch a shift at a job that is

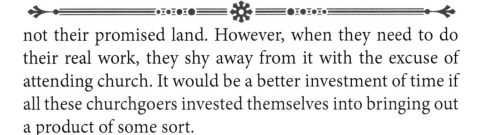

not their promised land. However, when they need to do their real work, they shy away from it with the excuse of attending church. It would be a better investment of time if all these churchgoers invested themselves into bringing out a product of some sort.

Perhaps you have had a dream that has been on your mind. There are too many of you sitting in pews in churches while the world cries out for the solutions that have been deposited in you. It could be a product to resolve the traffic problem in your country or city. Where is it? Why are you not working it? It could be a formula to resolve the corruption problem. The politics of the world, both in the developed and developing world, needs to be cleaned up by some altruistic leaders. Unfortunately, you spending all your time prostrating yourself in church to impress your pastor with your attendance record is not helping any of these issues.

Bill Gates left university to start his company Microsoft that became the biggest manufacturer of software for personal computers. Bill remarks now that he understood that the competition was only behind his idea for computer software by about 18-24 months. If he had delayed by staying in college and finishing his studies someone else would be the richest man on the earth today. This is a sobering thought when you think of all those ideas you have. Perhaps you delayed just a few months then out of somewhere a company comes out saying they have produced that same product or something extremely similar.

For Bill Gates, it was a formal university education that had the potential to hold him back, and for you, it may be church that is keeping you from producing something epic. This solution will bring glory to God. In fact, it will bring more glory to Him than ten years of going to church with no result. This is the essence of life. To be able to spread God's teachings and make life better for millions of people. This is a good way to use your time.

IT IS BETTER TO BE WORKING

It is better to be at work than to be pointlessly going to church. At least when you spend your time at work you are being compensated with something small for it. Wasting your time in church services that you cannot even recall what you learnt, is a dejected way to live. You were meant for a much better existence. Even though it is not the best use of your time, while working you receive a tiny bit of money in exchange. Going to religious activities from morning to night, on the other hand, does not have anything to show. You may get some goose bumps in some churches, that is all!

What did the early church spend their time on? The book of Acts in the bible chronicles these early days. In Acts 6, we see how the leaders of the church decided to prioritise what they did with their time:

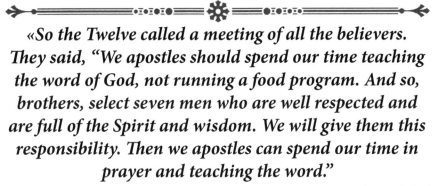

«So the Twelve called a meeting of all the believers. They said, "We apostles should spend our time teaching the word of God, not running a food program. And so, brothers, select seven men who are well respected and are full of the Spirit and wisdom. We will give them this responsibility. Then we apostles can spend our time in prayer and teaching the word."

Acts 6:2-4

As the early church grew by the thousands, the need to feed the widows arose and it happened that there was a quarrel over which race of widows were getting preferential treatment. The twelve apostles, who were the leaders at this crucial time, realised that the situation was asking them, What Do You Do With Your Time? They responded by differentiating between the work that God had called them to (praying and teaching the word) and what the church was demanding of them. We should also have this kind of attitude to be able to separate what God has asked of you and what your church culture is coercing you to do.

GREAT CHURCHES

Some readers of this book may now be thinking, «Pastor Sunday does not want people to attend church.» Let me extend to you an olive branch. If you attend a church that helps you by adding value to your life, then please make sure you are going. Does your church help you to get a fire of inspiration lit up in your belly? Then by all means go to that church as many times as you can.

Your time is being well invested when you attend churches like this because that adds value to you. If they encourage you after your week of giving everything into God's purpose for your life, that is exactly what we are looking for. There are churches out there, where the teachers give you incredible insight into how the word of God fits with what you do.

The preachers at these good churches unpack the bible stories in a way that releases understanding and revelation in your heart and mind. By this I am talking about knowing without doubt what the ancient texts mean and how they relate to your life today. These are true houses of God.

At times when the fire in you is waning a little bit, do the encouragers at church stoke the fire again? You need to get around these people. If church gives you a clear picture of how to do things better, if it equips you for service of God's Kingdom, if it gives you more ideas on how to fulfil your mission faster, then you need to be going with your pen and paper in hand. Get as much of that wisdom into you as you can. I am a big fan of a church that helps you with ideas on how to bring out the destiny that God put into you. Those that make you to achieve God's purpose faster than you do by yourself. When they assist you to see clearly into the Spirit of God, this a beautiful and relevant church. Do they make you see clearly into the mind of God? Do they make you to walk in more understanding?

The church I am describing here is what church should truly be. If your church is doing this for you, then you should be there all the time. There are too many good churches in your nation for you to not be attending a church that does these things for its congregants.

Are you a pastor reading this? I want to challenge you too. Does your church do the things that I described in the last paragraph for your members? If not, then why not? You are frustrating the children of God who are trying to do the best with the time He gave to them. Do not be surprised if they leave your church to find one that does bring out the best in them.

Let me get back to you, if you attend an amazing church. If your church does things that invest in you, you need to go there as many times as possible because that church is adding value to you. They are doing their own part by multiplying themselves as we spoke about. What that church is giving you is much more valuable in comparison to what you could be doing for yourself in that time. You should see it in terms of multiplying the value of your time and they will be doing that very well.

CHURCHES SHOULD BE DEDICATED TO ADDING VALUE TO YOU

When the church is dedicated to adding value to you, it means when you attend you are maximising your time. This is the right answer to our central question, What Do You Do With Your Time. Attending a church that adds value to you means you are walking in wisdom. When you do your comparative analysis of the things to be doing with your time, you realise that time you can be alone would be better spent getting things placed into your spirit and mind at church.

Comparative analysis is exactly the way that you tackle the decision as to what to do with your time compared to church attendance. Analyse and ask yourself, «If, with this time, I can write a whole book, even though it's Sunday today, will it be of more value than what they give me at church?»

"For the Son of Man is Lord of the Sabbath."

Jesus of Nazareth,
Matthew 12:8

Do not be afraid of the sacred traditions of your fellow church folk. Listen rather to what God recommends in the matter. God warned us against being swayed by the traditions of men. Church tradition defines Sunday as the Sabbath, but Jesus shows us, in the quote above, that He is

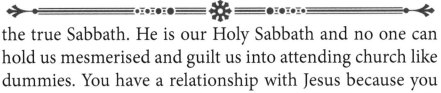
the true Sabbath. He is our Holy Sabbath and no one can hold us mesmerised and guilt us into attending church like dummies. You have a relationship with Jesus because you are in Christ. Do not let a day of the week be what controls you any longer. Do not let people manipulate you anymore.

If you are called to build wealth, the current dogma among charismatic Christians is to go to church and give large amounts of money to prophets and pastors. Wealthy non-Christians have habits that are far more helpful and you can take it to the bank. Here is a list of some of the things that millionaires do habitually while you go to church:

1. Maintain a to-do list.

2. Wake up three or more hours before they have to go to work.

3. Listen to audio books during their commute.

4. Network more than five hours each month.

5. Read at least 30 minutes each day.

6. Love to read.

7. Teach good daily success habits to their children.

8. Encourage their children to read more than two non-fiction books per month.

9. Watch an hour or less of TV every day and do not watch reality TV.

10. Focus on accomplishing a specific goal.

Take some time to do a comparative analysis of some of these habits with what you do with your time.

Let me summarise the ideas we explored in this chapter like this; By writing a whole book let us say while not going to church for a whole month, I have reproduced myself. I have not wasted that time, I have not spent that time but I have reproduced myself. I have invested my time into something else. I can hence show you what I have done with my Sunday. My life is being reproduced to actually bless many people but if I just go to church to sit every Sunday and there is nothing to show then I am a fool!

THE GOLDEN NUGGETS

1. Invest some of your church attendance time, especially if it is not being used in a productive manner.

2. Bring more glory to God with your time when you spend it finding solutions to problems. Attend church when it works out for you.

3. More glory comes to God from time in producing products instead of going through religious motions.

4. If your church is helping you along in your journey of fulfilling your destiny then make sure you attend whenever you can.

CHAPTER 7
CONVERSION OF
TIME

CHAPTER 7
CONVERSION OF TIME

In the last chapter, we explored how churches and the Christians who attend them can use their time in a better way. I had to address that particular group but now I would like to return to speaking in more general terms. In this chapter I will talk about what converting time looks like.

GARY CONVERTS HIS TIME

Gary Vaynerchuk is an entrepreneur famous for his work with social media. He is a highly-followed personality on Facebook, Twitter and Instagram as well as the CEO of Vayner Media, a digital marketing agency. Gary commands very high speaking fees for giving speeches and talks all over the world. He is also known for his no-filter, almost lack of respect for the status quo of the business world as he builds his dream. It is a well-known fact that he wants to buy the New York Jets, the American football team he has been a fan of since his family moved to America from Russia in the 1970s. To own an American football franchise will cost him multiple billions of dollars and the way Gary has used his time over the course of his career is an interesting thing.

As a young boy, Gary understood that he was not meant for school. His main skill was selling various things and so he had no interest in passing exams. At the age of 14, as he was already working to hone his salesman skills selling baseball cards in the malls of New Jersey, his father, in true immigrant fashion, put him to work in the liquor store that he had just bought. After a couple of years spent bagging ice in the basement he was let upstairs where he joined the salespeople. It was at this point that Gary Vaynerchuk saw that wine was something that people collected and that he had a chance to grow the family business very well. All the time that he was not in school he spent either selling in the store or reading about wine. In fact, he became the best wine salesman in the store long before he was legally allowed to drink.

While at college, Gary was introduced to the internet and while his friends saw a chance to get girls, he saw another way to sell wine. By this time, his father had recognized the gift of salesmanship that was in his son and so at the tender age of 24 he handed over the reins of operating Wine Library to Gary. Gary took practically no time off during his 20s. He passed on dating, hanging with friends and other fun things while he learned how to buy advertising, how to email market and trained his shop assistants.

At age 30, Gary's career took a turn for the better. Even though Gary Vaynerchuk was relatively successful, he had been realizing that his dream of buying the New York Jets would never come to fruition if he continued the way he was going. At this time, a little-known website by the name of YouTube was

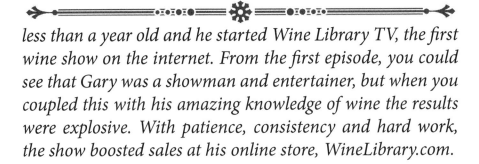

less than a year old and he started Wine Library TV, the first wine show on the internet. From the first episode, you could see that Gary was a showman and entertainer, but when you coupled this with his amazing knowledge of wine the results were explosive. With patience, consistency and hard work, the show boosted sales at his online store, WineLibrary.com.

Gary predicted that YouTube was going to be quite a big deal early and capitalized on it by selling a lot of wine. Another big turning point in his business career happened as he recognized that he had a knack for seeing what people's behavior online would be before it happened. This could be useful for more than selling wine. He spent time and effort taking a look at the technology business world and became one of the first investors in Twitter and Facebook. When these two investments blew up, it firmly placed Gary in the upper echelons of investors. His investment fund is one of the best performing around.

Gary Vee, as he became known, used his charismatic character to back up his business chops and become a renowned speaker now commanding a speaking fee in the six figures. He also hosts the Ask Gary Vee show, an internet video program where Gary answers different questions that are mainly about business and social media. Along with his younger brother, AJ Vaynerchuk, Gary has now decided to take the skills built over at least 20 years in business to start a social media agency called Vayner Media. This company is a major player in corporate America using a lot of the skills Gary used to build his personal brand to service large corporate clients like Pepsi, Johnson and Johnson and Budweiser.

Gary's plan to buy the New York Jets is simple enough. He keeps taking time to build practical businesses, which is what he is good at, and as he runs them he learns skills that allow him to grow to the next level. Consider that he started by growing his father's business from a $3 million turnover business to a $60 million one using email marketing, internet marketing and a video blog. With the knowledge he has accumulated, he now has an agency that makes hundreds of millions that does social media, digital marketing for the large corporations. The plan he has is to graduate by buying a major global brand for about $500 million and run it for a while before selling it for a few billion. Long term Gary Vaynerchuk wants to own the Jets but he also understands the role time has in the process.

From this story, I want you to look at Gary Vaynerchuk's actions and compare them with your own life. At age 16, Gary was converting his time to become the best wine salesman in the world. At age 30, he was converting his time into making himself the best video blog host in the world.

Can you use this same principle to turn your life mission into a reality? If you converted your time could you become a better doctor? Could you be a better inventor? Could you be a better musician? Do you convert time into anything that you want for your own life? What Do You Do With Your Time?

GOD'S PERSPECTIVE

What does God say about time? God, in the bible teaches us to maximise the time» because it is short.

«Making the best use of the time, because the days are evil.»

Ephesians 5:16 ESV

We need to be making the best possible use of the time we have. In the last chapter, I spoke about doing a comparative analysis of the value of what you are doing with your time. The reason given in the passage about this, is that the days are evil, according to Paul, who wrote the letter to the Ephesians. There are so many distractions nowadays that are being thrown in your path to get you to waste or spend your time in a way that is not productive to your calling. If Gary Vaynerchuk is meant to sell things to people in a way that leaves them satisfied and happy after every transaction, then that is what he is meant to be doing and he will feel fulfilled while doing it. It has nothing to do with going to heaven. Salvation is a different subject and that is between him and God.

Conversion of time is a practical thing. Every single day must be converted into a product of some sort. You must be able to look back each day and say, «Yesterday the product I created was this!» There are no hypothetical products and conversion is not philosophical. Execution

is the name of the game. If you cannot produce products, then you have failed to convert your day. This habit of daily conversion, is what adds up to create a successful life.

SHOW THE PRODUCT OF YOUR DAY

I challenge you to show concrete results. Show me the product of your day! This hour that has just passed, what is its product? Today, has there been anything you can point out as evidence? You will want to consider the past week as well. If you do not do this time will be running away from you while you are unaware. Write it down right now; over the past month, did you produce any value?

Take the example of 2 women who each have a business that deals in tailoring suits, there must be products that are used to measure how effective her business is. Examples of this could be how many suits do they sew, or how many suits are sold? A step further that is necessary would be the time in which this measurement is made. A finite time must be set to measure the suits sold.

So, if one woman sells ten suits in a month, she is more productive than the one who sells ten in a year. She makes more money, she can employ more workers and she gets better at her practice through working more.

As you apply this principle of converting your time into products in your own life, which of the two businesswomen in the example above would you like your life to resemble?

It must be the more productive one who makes and sells ten suits a month.

You need to create value in life. This is the measurement by which you must be accountable to yourself. Value can be looked at as the material or monetary worth of something. Looking at it this way, can you tell me what is the thing of material worth that you have created? Where is your value chain? When you assess the daily activities that you are involved in, they need to be leading up to the production of something of value. This is what I call a value chain.

How do you produce value for yourself on a daily basis? These enquiries need to be made of yourself. When life asks you these questions it will usually be more painful than if you ask them to yourself first. Take money for example. What do you do with your time to make money? As you ask yourself this, you may realise you are being lazy and unoriginal. A time will come however when as a young man, you want to get married. Life, through this particular situation, will be asking you the same question and if you cannot answer you will not be able to get married the way you wanted.

A lot of the people who follow me are glad that currently am doing a lot of work on my Facebook account. I have been recording messages on Facebook live twice a day. If you have not been listening to these then I urge you to find Dr Sunday Adelaja on Facebook and take a look at the videos on my 24-hour channel. When you watch me

daily at least you can point to that act of listening and say that is the value you are adding to yourself for that day.

Let me explain why this is great for you. When you watch and work through these videos on a daily basis, or you go to my YouTube channel and work through the different series I have, it is good because you are building yourself into a better man or woman. Examples of the series I have that you can convert are the Calling and Purpose series, the Work and Time series that this particular book is based on, and the series on Managing Finances. If you decided to take any of these series and seriously work through the information in them, you would be adding value to yourself. You would be making yourself better.

However, just working through the series is not enough. Listening alone is not sufficient. You have to then convert the materials and the wisdom in them into value which you are adding to yourself. Use them to make life changing decisions and take the action steps outlined in them to be a better person. You can also convert them into value added to other people. As I have pointed out before, this is a form of multiplying yourself in those other people.

«Knowledge will enrich you, but only action will turn it into riches!»

Dan McCormick,
American author and millionaire businessman

A millionaire and trainer of small businesspeople for over 30 years, Dan McCormick knows all about people who horde information yet do not apply it. It becomes useless. You are going to have to put the words you read into action to get results. The knowledge, understanding and wisdom that you get when you go through my materials and books are more than good. They have extraordinary nuggets stacked in them but unless you convert them that is all they will be. What you need to do with your time is you should then convert your time into adding value to products or produce certain products in the laboratory.

In summary, this chapter has been about showing that your time has to be converted into turning yourself to a person with value. This drive, to better yourself can be done with the materials, books and videos that I have, through rigorous study. In the next chapter, I will further explore what adding value with your time looks like.

THE GOLDEN NUGGETS

1. Maximize the time you have because it is short.

2. Everyday has to be converted into some sort of product. Show me that product in order to prove yourself.

3. Do you produce value for yourself on a daily basis? Do you listen to messages and train yourself?

4. To be complete, take what you have put in you and convert into value for others or products.

CHAPTER 8
HOW TO CREATE
VALUE IN YOUR DAY

CHAPTER 8
HOW TO CREATE VALUE IN YOUR DAY

In the last chapter I showed you how conversion of time works. In this chapter, I will be demonstrating to you some very practical ways in which you can create value, which is one of the best ways to convert your time.

BE PRESENT IN THE MOMENT

«When you want something you've never had, then you have to do something you've never done.»

Dr. Mike Murdock,
Author of "The Assignment"

We mentioned in the last chapter about the fact that you need to convert your day and must do this in a measurable way, you have to be adding value in that time frame. As the poignant words above say, you are going to do different things from here on if you want to get that value I talk about.

So, how do you create value in your day? This is getting deeper into what I recommend you start doing with your time. You need to be in the state of mind that allows you to create value. This is to say you need to be present in the moment and ready.

You are now almost halfway through this book. What have you gotten from me so far? Have you heard me loud and clear and are you really listening to me? How productive you become from now on is the proof that you have been listening to me. When you put this book down and you go to your job, to your ministry or to your business, you need to see how productive you truly are. There is the need to see real results shown. Visualise the product that you are going to produce tomorrow. Do you see anything? Get into a place where you can think alone if you need to in order to see in your mind the level of productivity that will come out of you.

I want you to take some practical steps right now in order to increase the value that you are getting. I believe that all humans know instinctively that their lives should produce something beneficial for mankind. As you read this book, there should be some things rising up on the inside of you that you feel need to come out as products. This is the effect of reading a book like this or going through my materials.

WHAT DO YOU FEEL INSPIRED TO PRODUCE?

The question above is the measuring stick you must use. How big have you become when it comes to your inner man? By this I mean do you feel like you have increased your ability to achieve new things? Your capacity to produce world changing products needs to have expanded. There must be an enlarging of what you feel like you can do.

King David, the second king of the nation of Israel, put the feeling this way,

«With your help, I can advance against a troop; with my God, I can scale a wall.»

Psalm 18:19

In this text, he is talking about the feeling he got when he had spent time in God's presence and the resulting value he felt had been deposited into him was that of wanting to take on a troop of enemy soldiers. It is important to note that David's career speciality was a warrior and soldier. So, the increase he felt pertained to feats of fighting. For you, it will be related to your own area of expertise.

If you are a musician, you may feel inspired to create new melodies and rhythms. For a lyricist or songwriter, you may have inspiration from a conversation you had with someone to pen something exciting and original. Are you

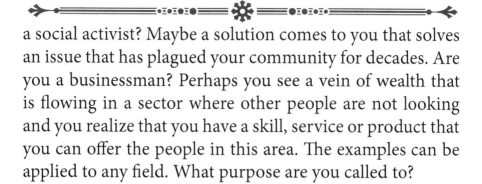

a social activist? Maybe a solution comes to you that solves an issue that has plagued your community for decades. Are you a businessman? Perhaps you see a vein of wealth that is flowing in a sector where other people are not looking and you realize that you have a skill, service or product that you can offer the people in this area. The examples can be applied to any field. What purpose are you called to?

Open yourself up to the possibilities this presents, because they are as endless as the thoughts of goodness God has for you. The vision you get should also be expansive. Do you see new things, new options and perceptions that you did not have before? This is proof that you are having value added to you by this book. Your lifestyle will also begin to change because when you see your current habits of poor productivity with your time, you cannot help but want to change.

George never reads books like this one anymore. As a result, he last got inspired to do something special when he was in school 20 years ago. George remembers how after he had been to the school library to research history and philosophy books he would feel inspired to think. This thinking was displayed when he was at Debate Club meetings. He shone more than any students there, presenting insightful arguments and besting his opponents.

Those glory days are long gone however. George is now a manager of a restaurant and has a family life that consumes his time. He feels like he leaves his genius at home

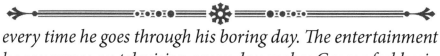

every time he goes through his boring day. The entertainment he consumes on television every day makes George feel brain dead. He wonders if he will ever feel as alive as when he used to do what he loved best.

Many people today live this kind of life. Do not be like George. Being brain dead and practically useless for God to use you in changing the world. This is basically the state that many people are in when they live an uninspired life. Read this book and do not ignore the inspiring feeling you get. Channel this into something that you love and use it to produce something tangible.

IF YOU STILL FEEL NOTHING

Maybe though, you are not seeing a change afoot. You perhaps are not truly feeling these things I am talking about. If you cannot see yourself producing anything it means you need to spend more time in the book or with the corresponding video materials. You may need to read the book again and again or if you learn better by listening to audio or video, then do that. Either way, you need to get these things into you. Deep down to the core of who you are, this wisdom has to immerse and penetrate your being. Dedicate and invest more time to studying, because your mind may just need to get more use to these information and concepts that are until now, fairly alien to it.

There is also another obstacle to learning and growing on the inside that you must contend with. This is the very real probability that wrong things have been added so far. In the same way that you are now adding value to your life remember that the reverse was true before now.

Vicky had a very negative family. Everything that was discussed in the house she grew up in was about putting someone else down. Her mother and sisters never seemed to talk about anything else other than what was going on in other people's lives and how they were better than the rest of their friends, family and neighbors.

Vicky only realized the negative effect of these things that had been constantly bombarded into her psyche when she left home. Her friends showed her how pessimistic she was and it made her difficult to be around. In order to change and learn to trust others, love others and be a better friend, Vicky is making an effort to spend time listening to people who she wants to be more like.

The world would be better off if people made such a deliberate effort to change the type of things that have entered our minds over the years. With more citizens being aware of the results on their actions of negative thinking there would be more people contributing to the economy of the nation and solutions to problems, than people wanting to take from the system.

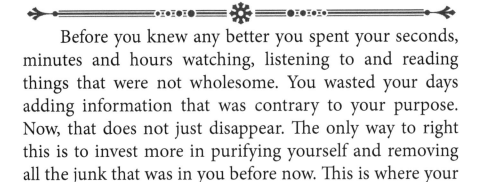

Before you knew any better you spent your seconds, minutes and hours watching, listening to and reading things that were not wholesome. You wasted your days adding information that was contrary to your purpose. Now, that does not just disappear. The only way to right this is to invest more in purifying yourself and removing all the junk that was in you before now. This is where your time needs to be spent initially.

There is a reason I tell you to do all this. It is in order for you to be able to take a hold and proper control of the direction your life is going. Your life until now has not been under your own control. You had been allowing it to move along on its own accord, affected by the mundane things that you spent your time on mostly before. In order to move on in a meaningful way, for you to be able to live out the things we are talking about, you need to expand what you are capable of. For you to be able to add value to others and to be able to produce tangible products that matter, you have to grow, and to spend necessary time clearing out the rubbish inside you.

GUARD YOUR TIME JEALOUSLY

For me I am very protective of my time. This is why I personally do not attend parties. People who come from my country, Nigeria, and especially those of my tribe, the Yoruba people, love to party for every occasion and if I attended all the parties I would be having little time to take hold of my life and my destiny. I only go when it is

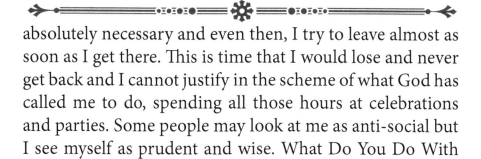

absolutely necessary and even then, I try to leave almost as soon as I get there. This is time that I would lose and never get back and I cannot justify in the scheme of what God has called me to do, spending all those hours at celebrations and parties. Some people may look at me as anti-social but I see myself as prudent and wise. What Do You Do With Your Time?

I can already here the questions, «So what do you do instead pastor?» I am always thinking and my mind is constantly alert for opportunities and chances to see what value can be produced in each moment. My awareness is hypersensitive to the prospects that I have to add value to other people around me. I compare this with the things that I am socially expected to do. I have gotten over the guilt that society tries to place on me and an obligation to be too social. If Nigerians, for instance, realised that some of these cultural pressures they feel to be at events, spending time and money can be overcome, we could change our nation and the communities that we live in abroad.

Our government should encourage our people to do as I do more often. I think, «What value could I have been producing in this party time?» Let us take the number of parties that happen in Lagos on a typical Saturday for example. If half the people who went to those parties did not go but did a comparative analysis of the value they could produce, the result would be tremendous. If they thought instead, "Can I do something today that will place a bit more money in my pocket for my family instead of spending my time and money at this party?" There would be a huge step in the right direction economically. Resources would not be wasted but would be acquired instead.

Apply this lesson to your life too. If you spend time to read books, you could have found out a concept that you were not aware of and then you can use it in the laboratory to create your ground-breaking product. Time spent studying would give you a new way to perform a task for your customers that would be very beneficial to them. You could also be researching more in order for the book that you are writing to have more weight to it.

In conclusion, there are practical things you can start doing now with your time that will give you value. This chapter has been about highlighting these things and challenging you to start doing them. In the next chapter, I will start giving you lessons on how I started converting my own time.

THE GOLDEN NUGGETS

1. How productive you become after reading this is the proof that you have heeded me.

2. Learn to increase your inner capacity and get bigger vision with what you have read.

3. If you cannot see yourself producing anything then it is an indication you need to spend more time investing in yourself. Study the materials some more and also take time to wash the junk that is already in you.

4. You must not spend time on trivial things like parties.

5. Do comparative analysis on the value that can be produced with each activity you are doing. You do this by asking, "Could I be producing a product?"

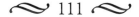

CHAPTER 9
HOW I STARTED
CONVERTING TIME

CHAPTER 9
HOW I STARTED CONVERTING TIME

In the previous chapter I explored with you the process of creating value using your time. To press this further and demonstrate even more practically, I am going to in this chapter tell you my own story. In the story of my life, you will begin to see how these principles came to life and got me to where I am today. May you, as you read, take this example and apply it into your own life. The story will weave in and out throughout the remainder of the book and I would like to help you understand conversion by sharing the story about how I started on the journey to converting time.

"Infinite striving to be the best is man's duty; It is its own reward. Everything else is in God's hands."

Gandhi

Mahatma Gandhi talks about the improvement that comes as a duty to men. As I tell you my story, this is truly what I used to become the man I became today.

YOUNG SUNDAY

At the age of 23, while I was still attending university in Russia, I knew intuitively that my life had to produce something measurable. I cannot explain the natural instinct that I had to this effect. To me, it was not right for a person to live aimlessly for any period of time, and there be no product to show for it. It was not natural. The course of things could not be for fruitlessness. There had to be fruit that could be assessed in any person's life. Do you feel this natural feeling too? Do you sense that there must be tangible things produced by your life?

The way I looked at it, God could not have taken me out of Nigeria, the country where I was born, for no reason. I sensed that I should do something tangible with my life. Speaking about it now it may seem obvious that I had this feeling. It is a dilemma that plagues many people, however, and if you consider the millions of people on earth who live without producing anything at all then you see it is not common for a young person to think like this.

Other great people who have felt this compulsion became great precisely because they followed the inclination to produce products. Take Pete Sampras for example. From an early age, Sampras wanted to compete and achieve things of note. For him, the extraordinary athletic abilities visible from an early age steered him into the word of tennis.

"Pistol Pete" Sampras became the first professional tennis player to break the previous record of 12 Grand Slam singles titles. He retired with 14 titles: seven at Wimbledon, five at the US Open, two at the Australian Open, a record only surpassed by Roger Federer in 2009. Sampras' other achievements include a record six ATP Player of the Year awards due to his ATP record No. 1 rankings from 1993 through 1998. He also won seven year-end championships five World Tour finals and two Grand Slam Cups.

It seems that Pete Sampras lived an example of how following the urge to produce something from your life can yield a reward of great life accomplishments. This is a concept that God Himself placed inside human beings. The urge you feel to achieve greatness is a God given clue to what we must do, and we must implement this in our schools and with our young people to steer them in the right direction of life. They will be much happier if we educate our children this way.

To sense that they need to be productive in life should be the first step for any person who desires to live a successful life. Young people have to see this in the older generation so that they will grow up understanding that this is a normal feeling. It is a sign of a country having it too good for too long when the children have been given so many distractions that come as presents from parents. Such is the way of life in the western world. You then find they never feel they need to produce anything with their lives.

According to the Nationwide's Christmas Spending Report that looked at how much parents spent on their children in the United Kingdom, it was shown that, on average, parents spend between £140 and £180 per child. This is just at Christmas. There has been a marked increase as the prosperity of families has generally increased. However, does this have to be at the expense of showing our children how to be counted among the productive in society. All these distractions, unfortunately, do not help our children.

It is of more use to our children if, like me, from an early age, we instil a sense of belonging to the national narrative and a sense that they have a part to play in it – a purpose.

THE INHERENT DESIRE TO PRODUCE

As I write this book I am glad that I have found the right words to describe what I felt as a young man because most of us do not. I think every human being is the same in sensing this. All of us sense it but whether life allows us an opportunity to do something about it is another question. There may be a young boy in India who feels his life should produce a result but unfortunately because he lives on the street in abject poverty he cannot follow his instinct. A young lady in an abusive family may be more occupied with protecting herself physically and mentally first before she explores how to produce products of value with her life.

Every human knows it deep down in their subconscious that they would like to do something with their life. Go through a first-grade classroom at any school up and down your country and you will see the glint of possibility in those little eyes. Count the members of parliament, the doctors, lawyers, pastors, teachers and scientists that are in that class. Note the number of cures for diseases, spaceships and palaces that are going to be discovered or built. The possibilities are endless when you ask children.

The story is told of a little girl who had never paid much attention in school. One day the teacher asked them all to draw a picture of anything they liked. When the teacher noticed, the little girl looking more engaged than she had ever been, she approached the girl's desk.

«What are you drawing?» she asked.

«A picture of God.» Came the reply.

«But nobody knows what God looks like.» Said the teacher.

Without lifting her eyes from the paper the girl said, «They will in a minute!»

The point of this story is that kids do not have a limit to what they think is possible in life. We only seem to grow out of this character as we get older. In the same way children have an inherent desire to produce spectacular things with their lives.

The feeling I had as a young man starting out is not only limited to me. Everybody feels that they would like to add value in some way. They may feel the need to add value to themselves, to add value to others or to add value by producing products. We would all like to bring something to fruition that people can look at and say, «This is what you brought into existence.» Possibility is surely endless as we think, "Is it too much, to ask for that; I add value to the world in my own small way?"

People do have a need of wanting their life to matter. We would all like our life to matter, perhaps by writing or making something that means something to someone else. We would like to bring forth results and to be of benefit to mankind somehow. Maybe an invention that comes out of you, heals thousands who had been condemned to death. Perhaps a policy you think up becomes the legislation that protects children around the country. We all have this need as brilliantly put by the author below:

«God gave you a supercomputer in your head. The conscious area of the brain processes 2000 transactions per second. The limbic area (the heart and subconscious mind) of your brain 400 billion per second. Don't take that and just live an ordinary life!»

Steven K Scott,
Author of Success God's Way

Do you even use a fraction the power of the supercomputer inside your cranium? Researchers and scientists still admit we do not fully understand what the brain is capable of. You must therefore start today to use your time to uncover how you can start taking advantage of your hidden power.

PRODUCING SOMETHING MEASURABLE

To continue with my story, what I did next in my twenties is decide to measure my life by what product I produced with every passing year. The key here was the word MEASURE because this is what was the difference between me and others. You cannot improve something that you have failed to measure. This is the basis of the scientific method of doing things. I had to find a way that the products I wanted out of myself could be counted. This was important to me as I wrote down what I wanted to achieve.

Here is the way I did it. I said to myself, «Today is my 23rd birthday. I want to do something between now and my 24th birthday.» This defined a measure of time, which denoted my getting older would be particularly powerful because on one's birthday more than any day you feel that your life is running out. I would be a year older which would be a good reminder to keep going and keep producing.

What did I want to achieve? I wanted to do something in that year so that at the end of the year I could hold

something up and say, «Yes I have produced this!» I know it may seem small compared with all that I was saying in earlier chapters about assessing what you do with your time by a maximum day package. Remember however, that this is how I started. I am totally different now but it will give you hope if you felt like you could never get to producing products on a daily basis.

SIMPLY START SOMEWHERE

We all need a place to start. It is very important that you do not take on too much initially, and that you do not set unrealistic goal for producing products. At 23, what I did was a good start for me. Right now, I laugh out loud when I think about it, but it was something that I could handle at that time. I want to warn you not to take on more than you can chew when the urge to get going hits you. In the last chapter I spoke about the great reaction that happens as you go through the book. You just need to be a bit careful on how you take on the tasks to produce. You can start slowly at first.

What is the point of all of this? It is about learning how to measure your life. This you can only articulate by showing what your life has been able to produce in a year.

When my 24th birthday arrived, I had work to do. I looked hard for something that I could count. This was very important. Remember I just pointed out the crucial step, that whatever you are doing must be measurable. This

is what I recommend you do as well. Count and measure your results routinely. Make it a habit.

My initial results were not anything to write home about. Since I was not purposeful I just hoped that there was something that had happened. I got to my birthday and racked my mind to even produce some little bit of a result. What things could I count? What had I done, in reality?

INITIAL RESULTS

The things I counted that initial year will make you laugh. When I tried to recall, I thought perhaps I had managed to read some books. There were a few Christian books I counted as well as some that were on my university course. I did not know that those books that were on my course did not really count. They were already recommended reading for the degree course I was taking at the time, so I cannot say they were a product I produced.

Another thing I counted was the fact that I had managed to graduate, the year that I was studying for my degree. I had managed to go from one class to the next! This is something that happens automatically in university so I say it does not count either. If you just followed the natural course of life, that graduation would happen anyway. Therefore, in my estimation, it should not be counted as a product.

How mistaken young Sunday was! Most of these things were not products that were proof of my life. Compared to the products I produce now like books, videos, churches and businesses, I had just spent a whole year and I had no proof for my life. The only thing I could point to was that I was still a Christian. This was time spent and definitely not in the best way. The fact that I had moved from a year to another in my studies was just automatic and almost everyone else was doing the same. That is not a product. This was all that I had done with my time.

To conclude this chapter, my start was not very encouraging. Do not despair though, because things got better. In the next chapter I will get into how I started improving and what I started to consider as products worthy to be counted.

THE GOLDEN NUGGETS

1. As a young man, I knew I needed to produce products of some kind. I did not start quickly.

2. Every human feels the same urge to produce.

3. My first goal was to produce a product each year.

4. At the end of that first year, I had read some books, graduated in my university course. I thought I had done much but now I realize I was counting things that happen automatically. I was not intentional.

CHAPTER 10
INVESTING IN
PRODUCTS

CHAPTER 10
INVESTING IN PRODUCTS

In the last chapter, I showed at length what I did as I started producing products. As a continuation of my story, let me take time to define further and explain what investing in products looks like.

WHAT ARE YOUR PRODUCTS?

A product is defined in the dictionary as, "an article or substance that is manufactured or refined for sale". I have earlier in the book been describing products as, "something tangible that you come up with in the laboratory which is valuable". I like the dictionary definition because it implies that you can get money for your product if it is of a high enough standard. This shows you the advantage and reward that God gives you for investing your time wisely in producing products.

When you go to a job you are producing products of value in one way or another. These products have a monetary value but you have no part in harvesting that value. You have already been compensated through your wages and your employer is the one who now owns the value of those products. The company is your employer's promised land, not yours.

A product, as I define it here, is something you have been intentional about producing, not just something that happens with the natural flowing of life. Natural occurrences like the logical stages of life, getting married, having children, are not included in what we are counting here.

On January 9, 2007 Steve Jobs stepped on the stage to give one of the most incredible keynote presentations of his life and in the history of consumer electronics. He said he would be introducing a wide-screen iPod with touch controls, a revolutionary mobile phone, and a breakthrough internet device. But it was not in the form of three products. It was one product. It was the iPhone.

It was rare enough for a company to revolutionize even one product category. Apple had already revolutionized two: Computers with the Mac and personal music players with the iPod. With the iPhone, they would be going for three.

First, Steve Jobs set up and knocked down the physical keyboard and the screen pointing pen, features that dominated the BlackBerry, Motorola, and Palm smartphones of the day. Then he introduced the multitouch interface that let the iPhone smoothly pinch-to-zoom, the physics-based interactivity, and the multitasking that let him move seamlessly from music to call to web to email and back.

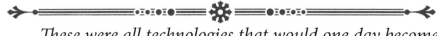

These were all technologies that would one day become commonplace across the industry but back then looked like science fiction. Apple released this statement:

"iPhone is a revolutionary and magical product that is literally five years ahead of any other mobile phone. We are all born with the ultimate pointing device—our fingers—and iPhone uses them to create the most revolutionary user interface since the mouse."

The iPhone still is one of the most important products of this young century. It was one of the pivotal products Apple. There is an important lesson that can be learnt by our countries in this example. You may not have the next iPhone in your mind, but you never know what you are capable of until you get producing. There must be a value of productivity implemented in our companies such as Apple had, when they produced the iPhone. Just as it has created billions of dollars in revenue for the company, if we produce consistently as a nation, our GDP will go up and we will sustain our economies.

WHAT DOES NOT COUNT AS PRODUCT?

"Not everything that counts can be counted, and not everything that can be counted counts."

Albert Einstein

Let us look closely at what counts as products. As Albert Einstein observed, just because something is there, does not mean we must automatically count it without scrutiny. When I speak of investing in products I am not talking about the routine things of life. Look at something like a dog, a pig, a cat or a bird. These are creatures that wake up every morning like clockwork. They go on to live their day driven by a few basic impulses: the impulse to eat, to find shelter, to breed and to avoid death.

I am ashamed to say that too many people live this same way. You are not a dog and you are not a bird! I hope that making these strong comparisons will jolt you out of inaction into producing products. Ask yourself today why you have not intentionally produced anything with your life. What were you given the life for? What Do You Do With Your Time?

Take this example of someone who is living their life by impulse. A child is sent to school where he goes through all the courses that his parents want him to. The next step is that he goes to university to study a degree course that he has been told has a high chance of yielding a high paying job. At university, he meets a girl from his home town and in line with cultural norms, they fall in love and get married as soon as they graduate.

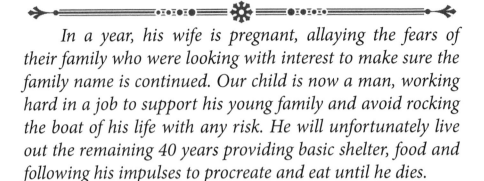

In a year, his wife is pregnant, allaying the fears of their family who were looking with interest to make sure the family name is continued. Our child is now a man, working hard in a job to support his young family and avoid rocking the boat of his life with any risk. He will unfortunately live out the remaining 40 years providing basic shelter, food and following his impulses to procreate and eat until he dies.

Living like a simple animal, like the man in the example above, is a terrible way for your life to pass. It means that your life keeps on reducing. Consider our original image of your existence as a jar filled with water. Every day that you are foraging around seeking nothing but survival, you are pouring more of your life out of the jar. This means you have less left. All this is happening with no result to be seen. You are living a wasted life and this is the saddest thing. Men and women who lived before you would be envious of this time in history that you are alive. The twenty first century is an exciting moment in history where a lot of things have converged to make living a great life possible. The kind of products that you can now produce are of better quality and quantity than what Winston Churchill, for example, had to work with. Living the life of an animal is not doing it justice.

Do not be like me in my first year of measuring my products. I would measure things I thought counted but they were a waste of life. Graduating to the next year, still being saved, these were all useless measurements of productivity that I mistakenly thought counted.

EARLY SIGNS OF PROGRESS

So, how did I get better at producing products? It took work and a concerted effort as I invested into myself and added value to me. As I grew I started learning and getting wisdom on these matters. I made a discovery that was monumental for me, and this was the fact that a person did not get to producing great products by mistake. It was not something that happened by chance or coincidentally. When I got the power of intentionality, I started to wilfully make sure that I really produced a proper product every year. The joy I felt when I managed to do this was something you would not understand. I had gotten to my target.

I found that the first time producing deliberate products was the hardest. After this I started measuring myself based on the products I produced within the span of a year. This became the benchmark that I used to count the products of my life. The question was no longer about IF I could produce a product but HOW MANY could I have that year.

Learning this skill in your youth will be a useful skill for you in your life. You will not be misled by the smokescreen that the world system sends your way where they congratulate you for mundane animalistic achievements like having a baby, graduating from a class in school and such like. Do not get me wrong and stop celebrating your children's birthdays. However, you need to become aware enough to see past these pointless distractions and look closely at your true product that year.

The challenge I present to you is, "Do you a have product you can point to that you produced over the last year?" Write it down. Be truly honest with yourself. If you can answer this question, then you are going in the right direction with your life. What Do You Do With Your Time? Is there anything in your home, in your shop or any shop for that matter, on a website, in your church? Is there something you can point to and say, «This is the product I produced over this last year!»

James, the first bishop of the first church in Jerusalem, challenged Christians who claimed they had faith in God but had no actions to show for it:

What good is it, dear brothers and sisters, if you say you have faith but don't show it by your actions? Can that kind of faith save anyone?

Suppose you see a brother or sister who has no food or clothing, and you say, "Good-bye and have a good day; stay warm and eat well"—but then you don't give that person any food or clothing. What good does that do? So, you see, faith by itself isn't enough. Unless it produces good deeds, it is dead and useless.

Now someone may argue, "Some people have faith; others have good deeds." But I say, "How can you show me your faith if you don't have good deeds? I will show you my faith by my good deeds."

You say you have faith, for you believe that there is one God. Good for you! Even the demons believe this, and they tremble in terror. How foolish! Can't you see that faith without good deeds is useless?

Don't you remember that our ancestor Abraham was shown to be right with God by his actions when he offered his son Isaac on the altar? You see, his faith and his actions worked together. His actions made his faith complete. And so, it happened just as the Scriptures say: "Abraham believed God, and God counted him as righteous because of his faith." He was even called the friend of God.

So, you see, we are shown to be right with God by what we do, not by faith alone. Rahab the prostitute is another example. She was shown to be right with God by her actions when she hid those messengers and sent them safely away by a different road. Just as the body is dead without breath, so also faith is dead without good works.

James 2:14-26 NLT

The question the author asked here is poignant. What good is faith without works? It reinforces what we have been discussing about producing products. The only proof that you have faith is in the actions or products you produce. So, it is with your time. The only proof that you have done something with it is in real products.

To conclude, we showed in this chapter that asking yourself honest questions about the products you produce is one of the ways you can keep yourself accountable as to what you do with your time. In the next chapter I will be demonstrating how I continued to increase the rate at which I converted time into products.

THE GOLDEN NUGGETS

1. A product is something you are intentional about producing.

2. Some things that even animals and birds can do automatically like reproduce and get on with their lives do not count as products in my opinion.

3. Mundane things just reduce your life without any tangible results.

4. As I grew in wisdom I became focused and made sure I produced one product a year.

5. What can you point to that you produced over the last year?

CHAPTER 11
HOW I IMPROVED
MY CONVERSION
RATE

CHAPTER 11
HOW I IMPROVED MY CONVERSION RATE

In the last chapter I started to show how you to assess the products that you create with your time. In this chapter I will continue in that same vein but I will be showing you through the practical example of my own life. I will show you how to start slow until you are seeing definite results as well as how to improve your results.

SLOW DELIBERATE STEPS

"Life is not long, and too much of it must not pass in idle deliberation how it shall be spent."

Dr. Samuel Johnson,
18th Century British literary critic

In chapter 9, I started telling you about how I got started on the journey to converting my time into products. Even though I did not know them at the time, the words of Dr. Samuel Johnson describe the development process I went through. As you saw it was not a quick start by any means. In fact, I started very slowly compared to what I do now.

This improvement and how I managed it is what I'm going to get into now and I believe there are lessons in this story that you will be able to take into your own world right now.

You must see the underlying principle that being consistent with action over a period of time will yield results for you. It may not be obvious at first but it is undeniable. A toddler who is in a hurry to grow up fails to see the growth he is going through because of impatience. His parents however are noticing his height increase and his features changing. Before you know it, he is a teenager wondering where the simpler days went.

In the same way, you need to commit yourself to the process of growth. Wherever you start, maybe you were wasting time or you were spending it on things that you thought were of value, just remember you are going to be in a process of changing, and it may take time. This is the very thing this book is based on. You must invest your time in growing yourself until you can produce more.

I started maturing in wisdom regarding who I was. I was working hard to become better as a young church leader and young man, and was spending time getting educated until I got to a place in my life where I could direct, in a much better way, where I was going. This took a lot of work but you must know it is possible to get there. By striving earnestly, you can get the understanding you need to be able to get to where you could begin to measure your life. This is exactly what happened to me.

This was what Paul of Tarsus, the early church father, spoke to his young apprentice Timothy when he said,

«*Be diligent to show yourself approved to God, a workman who does not need to be ashamed, accurately dividing the word of truth.*»

2 Timothy 2:15

The words «be diligent» can be translated work hard or be studious or study. There needs to be a deliberate, consistent effort to improve yourself when you want to become more productive. The deliberate part means no one else can do it for you. If you want muscles, you have to go to the gym. If you want to be wise you have to get knowledge. The consistency element is what usually eludes most of us who have mastered the first part. Consistency intensifies the effect of what you are building in yourself.

Take compound interest, for instance. This is where money accruing with a compounded interest becomes very substantial with time. If you invested $10 a month over 30 years, with an annual interest of 30%, here is what it would look like:

Year	Total Deposits	Year Interest	Total Interest	Balance
1	$120	$18.72	$18.72	$138.72
10	$1,200	$1,351.05	$4,712.15	$5,912.15
20	$2,400	$20,159.65	$85,016.10	$87,416.10
30	$3,600	$279,452.23	$1,207,417.25	$1,211,017.25

It is interesting what happens with time to the total interest that one earns on their money and consequently the total balance they have. In the first year, they only have $138.72 but after 30 years of letting the interest accrue and build up they have more than a million dollars!

Consistency over time is the crucial part of all this, and it is the same with building your skills and knowledge over time.

The other part Paul brings up in the quote above is that when you study you show yourself as a workman who does not have to be ashamed. You must «show» yourself. The results must be tangible. I was ashamed after my results in my first year, not just in front of other people, but in my own heart as I knew God was watching me. The products that you can point to mean that you can never be shamed by anyone. When they ask, What Do You Do With Your Time, you have an answer you can show!

STUDY AND WORK HARD TO GET BETTER

Studying helped me get better. It occurred to me one day that if I could do what I had done in a year and produce on product, with more intention perhaps I could have two products to show by my next birthday. One product turned out not to be that hard to produce in reality. If one product could be done like that with relative ease, then two was equally possible.

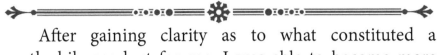
After gaining clarity as to what constituted a worthwhile product for me, I was able to become more focussed about what I produced. So, those earlier things I mentioned last chapter, which were not really products no longer took up my time. Things like whether I was still a Christian or not. As I understood that graduating to the next level of my university course was a good thing but I was not counting it as a product, I could focus the necessary time to it and make adjustments with activities that produced a real product. This is the power of focus. Removing unnecessary distractions was a big help to me.

I want to also challenge you about releasing the seal of unbelief that may be affecting your mind. When you first hear these concepts about products, you may get discouraged because you have not produced real products in weeks, months or even years. Perhaps you may be thinking, «It is too late for me.» You feel if you had heard this before you wasted time then maybe you could do something. Taking your first step and producing one product will show you that anything is possible. It releases you from shackles of your mind. After one product is produced you say to yourself, «What was I scared of? It is actually not as scary as I made it out to be!» Then you are chopping at the bits, ready to produce more. Embrace this feeling of faith and possibility. I did! You too can.

As I grew and developed, I started to organise my life on purpose to be able to move forward to having two products in a year. I brought in processes to protect me

from distractions. I scheduled activities that would help me attain my goal. The end result had become that every six months I had a product.

PLANNING YOUR PRODUCTS

Hollywood studios and producers have become quite good at planning the products they want to make and sell. The change that has occurred in the 21st century has a lot to do with this. The most popular Hollywood blockbusters these days tend to be franchises based on books, comics or video games. There is a lot of business value in nostalgia in the current economy.

A case in point is the Marvel Avengers, X-Men, Guardians of the Galaxy and Spider-Man franchises that are currently popular. Marvel has already produced multiple films that have made them billions of dollars.

The two Avengers movies we have had so far have introduced us to the characters Iron Man, Captain America and Thor. X-Men's Wolverine has been very popular as well. What I would like to bring your attention is how they have slowly been producing movie after movie at the rate of about one a year. With the popularity of these movies, the studio is going to the almost infinite vault of stories that is the Marvel Multiverse and they are now planning movies at much more regular intervals. With each movie, they introduce another character who will appear in his or her own movie at a later date.

Now with Black Panther, they have introduced the world to the first African hero to capture that market more. Doctor Strange and Captain Marvel will also be new movies all planned for the next five years and longer. This is a prudent amount of planning so they make sure they have resources lined up by the time they get to producing the movies. This kind of thinking is now being deployed by DC Studios and other large studios as they cope with, the drop in box office sales. We can learn a lot from how they do this.

Why are we letting the Hollywood use this principle of the kingdom of God while we do not? Planning our products is a secret from God that we must use in all our lives once we realize what area of purpose He created us for. When you know what you want to produce, then like these studios, plan the steps that you will take to achieve what you want. If you have an idea, how about breaking it up into a series of products that you can get out at regular intervals? This is the lesson from the Hollywood movie studios of today.

As my own methodology for producing products improved, I began to be able to produce three products per year. Then it went up to four. The kind of products that were relevant to me included books that I was writing, churches that were being built and people who were being helped by our church activities. Being able to produce a product in every quarter that went by was a great achievement for me.

I saw that once you get going with producing products, then improvement tends to get easier. On the other hand, if you never get to that start point of one product a year then you are dead in the water. When a machine that churns out products is working well, then it appears seamless when multiple products are coming out the other end. The really hard work of creating that machine initially is what people do not speak about. Let me offer this challenge to you: Where are the products of your life?

I would like to also tell you about a lady who is improving her own productivity. This is Pat and she is in Australia. Pat writes and makes documentaries about mental health issues that the poor experience. She is a talented filmmaker and several years ago she went through episodes where she was afflicted with schizophrenia. At the time, she thought she was never going to get better but as she began to combine what she was good at with the strong emotions she felt towards the challenge of mental illness, she has been living like a woman on a mission.

The first documentary she made took Pat two years to go from writing the script to the finished product. She was not happy with this because she had a limited number of films she could make in the remainder of her life. So, she devised systems to try and improve. Pat broke down the process of making her documentaries into its component parts.

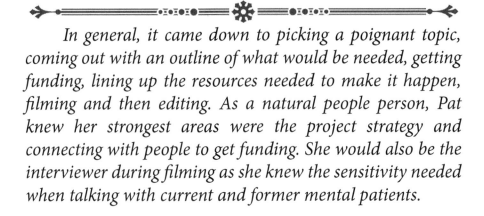

In general, it came down to picking a poignant topic, coming out with an outline of what would be needed, getting funding, lining up the resources needed to make it happen, filming and then editing. As a natural people person, Pat knew her strongest areas were the project strategy and connecting with people to get funding. She would also be the interviewer during filming as she knew the sensitivity needed when talking with current and former mental patients.

Everything else she needed was outside help and partners. When she put these in place for her next film it only took a year to complete. Now that she has her dream team in place and has ironed all the teething problems inherent in working with a new team, she produces her documentaries in four months and can spend the rest of the year promoting her work and getting many more people to see it.

I want to challenge you to improve your own personal productivity by applying this concept like Pat. She is a shining example of someone who is working well to self-improve.

To summarize this chapter, I used small steps to get better at bringing out tangible products from my life. It took a lot of hard work and deliberate action. In the next chapter, I will look at how you can live a life of near-perfect productivity.

THE GOLDEN NUGGETS

1. I matured to a point where I could improve my producing.

2. If I could do a product in a year, with more intention about it, I could do even more.

3. I began to organize my life to be able to double my productivity.

4. I could only get better and produce three then four products a year.

CHAPTER 12
LIVING A
PRODUCTIVE LIFE

CHAPTER 12
LIVING A PRODUCTIVE LIFE

In the last chapter, I showed how I improved the way that I produced the amount of products I was producing. In this chapter I will show you how to use regular assessment to improve the quality and quantity of what you are producing.

PERFECT PRODUCTIVITY

Consider Jesus Christ for a moment. It is my opinion that he is by far the most productive person who ever lived and I will show you why I believe this. Of course, you can argue He was the Son of God and had superpowers but let me show you how this is the wrong assessment of His life. The time of His ministry or work on earth was about three and a half years. Yet the products He produced in that time were of such quality and quantity that we still talk of His legacy 2000 years later.

Let us look at His first 30 years. The bible tends to speak only of the events leading up to His birth, a brief account of how He was born and what transpired immediately after. We get a few sentences on His infancy in exile in Egypt until He was around three then a fun interlude of Him at age 12. After this, in all canonical accounts of Jesus' life,

He re-appears aged 30 rearing and ready to take His life mission by the horns.

Why is there a gaping hole in the story? Surely if He had such a powerful life then we should hear of His teen years and early twenties. This is not the case and I believe there is a lesson very relevant to this book that can be gleaned from this.

The importance of time in God's plan is evident in the recorded life of Jesus. God could have brought Him to prominence ready to go. He did not have to place Jesus in the family of a carpenter from Nazareth. This, however, would not have been a good example so God in His infinite wisdom wanted us to see that if His Own Son needed to spend time in obscurity brooding over the word of God and having wisdom expand inside Him. In fact, in the only statement given after Jesus' funny episode at age 12 in Jerusalem was that, «...the boy grew in stature and wisdom...»

Jesus shut Himself away learning how to tell stories, learning how to deal with people, learning about His enemies, getting to understand the Torah (Jewish bible) from which He would preach and teach and learning how to lead men. He took time to study the financial system, the government system of the day, his trade as a carpenter, how to relate with children and how to debate belligerent opponents. Jesus used His time to grasp how to prophesy, how to perform miracles, how to serve His friends, how to

socialise and most importantly how to connect with His Father in prayer.

In Jerusalem, 12-year-old Jesus went missing for 3 days but his parents found Him in the temple. He was questioning the teachers of the law. He saw the need to find out more about His specialist subject matter. After all, in 18 years' time, He would be teaching that stuff incredibly well. Jesus was humble enough to spend time with the teachers of His day, even though we know He ended up bringing the message that completed the law of Moses. Therefore, I am challenging you to get in solitude with God and the materials that pertain to your calling.

The results Jesus produced are to this day unparalleled. The words He spoke were immortalised in four books in the bible and are talked about and preached on by over a billion people on the planet every day. The things He did have revolutionised the way we humans treat others ever since. He is the benchmark of kindness and charity for every nation and organisation. Also, the men and women that He trained up turned the world upside down and set up the longest running, biggest and most diverse organisation in the history of the world – the Christian Church.

That right there, is producing products! Through Jesus Christ we know what ultimate productivity looks like.

ASSESS YOURSELF

Have you started living a productive life yet? You could be at the point that I was at 23 or you could be a little further along. You could even be below that point.

"Courage is the most important of all the virtues because without courage, you cannot practice any other virtue consistently."

Maya Angelou

Poet and icon Maya Angelou talked about the courage that makes it possible for us to be truly virtuous. This kind of courage will be essential as you assess how productive you have been. Taking a self-evaluation will be uncomfortable and will be a pain staking exercise. However, as you do this, you will discover yourself first by figuring out if there is anything you could point out that you have produced. So, take a page out of Maya Angelou's book and get it done.

What are you doing with your time? What products can you show? We are not counting the instinctive things of life like sleeping with a woman and getting her pregnant. The things that animals of lesser intelligence than the human race also do like producing young do not count as products in this assessment. You have to look at those things that you do deliberately.

Here is where to start. Could you take an inventory of your life? In the areas that you are gifted. What did you do last year with the gift of preaching that you have.

Dan is a Zimbabwean who lives in the UK. From a young age, he realized he had a mind different to most people. A critical thinker, he looks at problems, issues and ideas and comes up with innovative ways to solve them. The main areas Dan is interested in are business and faith.

At first, he worked a job in IT and occasionally his church would invite him to teach. They saw his giftedness, but could only invite him a couple of times. Dan tells the story of coming across what I am talking about with regards to converting time. He says it put into words what he had been doing for the past couple of years without knowing. These are his words,

«My breaking point came when my wife and I separated. She complained that I was a man of too many ideas and too little action. One of the reasons she had liked me initially was my Godly vision and ideas but after years of marriage there was no product to show for it. Being in this place of desperation made me retreat in prayer so I could learn how to produce products. I found out I had invested so much in myself over the years but was not in turn taking that and adding value to others or providing a product or service that I could sell.

"People had started telling me I inspired them with my daily posts on Facebook. I started being more consistent by producing a video and a blog post every week that was linked to my daily posts on Facebook and Instagram. I used my natural writing and teaching talents but also started spending time getting better at social media and business. Soon I met people who wanted to work with me. Now I have started a company that offers services that help businesses sell more and individuals make money on social media. I have a community of online entrepreneurs who visit my Instagram, Facebook and blog pages daily looking for motivation and inspiration. Also, I am currently writing my first book!»

Dan is one of a growing number of people who are producing products using the exposure that the internet can give. Could you, like him, begin to live an intentional life? If everyone keeps commenting on your good ideas but you do not have much to show for it, then you are going to need to start being purposeful now.

START TODAY, START NOW

"Change will not come if we wait for some other person or some other time. We are the ones we have been waiting for. We are the change that we seek."

Barack Obama

You can start today. Perhaps it is worth you starting with small assessments. Rome may not have been built in a day but they started somewhere after all. You may be thinking, «Pastor I am not like you in my execution and I am definitely not at Jesus' level!» That is fine. You have just seen me show you in the last chapters that neither was I. The key to getting there someday is to start by measuring yourself with the type of goals that you can realistically achieve. The younger and less experienced you are, the better because you have a long way to go.

People use the expression, "I am so hungry I could eat a horse." However, if you actually went ahead with eating a horse, you would quickly realise just how big it is and perhaps you were not that hungry after all. If you say you are going to produce 24 products in the next 24 hours, then I guarantee you will fail and be burnt out before you get going.

How do you start instead? Let us set an arbitrary start point of using yearly assessments. Like I did, you can start by giving yourself one year to produce your product. You may use a memorable day like your birthday or wedding anniversary. Perhaps doing it from the first of January works better for you. The secret to success is choosing something that will keep you accountable as well as excited. The long-term goal will be to get to a place where every day is being converted into a product. This is where you will get eventually, but for now a product a year is a good place to start if you are currently producing none.

The progression I made from one product a year to two, three and eventually four was an achievement I am glad took place. The process helped me in many ways and grew me immensely.

In this chapter, we looked at the ultimate example of perfect productivity, Jesus Christ. In the next chapter, we will explore the lessons I have personally learnt on conversion.

THE GOLDEN NUGGETS

1. When you assess yourself honestly, have you started living a productive life yet?

2. Take an inventory of your life. Could you start being productive.

3. Jesus was the epitome of productivity. His three and a half years of working were better than most of us do in 40 years.

4. Set yourself goals and targets on the products you want to produce.

5. You start at the level you can handle, whether it is a product a year or a product a month.

CHAPTER 13
LESSONS ON
CONVERSION FROM
MY LIFE

CHAPTER 13
LESSONS ON CONVERSION FROM MY LIFE

Last chapter, I threw out the challenge for you to start living the productive life now! And one of the best ways to do this is to start converting your life into value. This value can be in the form of value in yourself, in others or in the form of products and services. In this chapter I will go through the lessons I learnt on conversion.

TAKING MY PRODUCTIVITY TO ANOTHER LEVEL

The previous few chapters I have given you a lot of the way that I learnt how to convert my time into value and products. There were many lessons in there and some of them I am going to summarise here as I conclude everything. I aim to conclude all into a neat package for you.

How did this process work for me? Through growing and learning, God helped me to take my productivity to the next level. I spent a lot of time at His feet getting information and using it to expand my own capacity to do big and great things. By this statement, I mean I purposefully spent time in prayer and meditating on the teachings of God I

have come to understand in my Christian life. I was also seeking and searching many areas that I could to add value to myself.

I searched the bible. As a pastor, a lot of the products I produced needed me to know God's word to a level where I could sift through truth and present it to people. I had to accurately divide the word of truth. I was seeking through books of inspiring leaders.

In order to write my own books like this one, I put a lot of research and work into finding inspiring stories of leaders in every sector of society. Books on business, politics, national histories, other pastors, I spent a lot of time in all of them.

TRAINING MYSELF

"What you keep between your eyes will affect you."

Joel Osteen,
Author of Your Best Life Now

Like the author here puts, I needed to be careful what I put in front of myself. I had to train myself. In my circle, very few people were doing what I knew God had called me to do. Especially in my part of the world there were few who looked like me and were producing the calibre products that I wanted to. I had to condition myself to get to the level I needed. You need to, in the same way, be working on yourself.

When I ask you the question what do you do with your time I am also asking you to recognise that no one else has the responsibility for your life and to produce your results. When you stand before God only you will be able to answer Him about the talents you were given. The question is not for your church, for your family or for your nation alone. It is for you.

Having this individual responsibility is good for the collective group though. If every member of your church, for example, understands what I am saying and begin to live by these same principles I'm telling you right now, the products produced will enrich your church in many ways. People will be maturing on a daily basis, money will not be an issue and families will be strengthened.

You can see from what I said that products did not just appear because I sat down and did nothing. By seeking and searching I started to intentionally bring out results. Do you know why «Get Rich Quick» schemes are so successful for the people who devise them? You would think in a 21st century world where people have heard all about these things no one would ever sign up for one. But no. These schemes keep signing up many people. The people who come up with the schemes make quite a large amount of money from them.

The main reason this all happens is because there is still a large number of people who just want to do the least amount of work and get a big result. There is always

someone who wants a result without doing anything and unfortunately that person will continue to have their money taken. You, like I was, have to be willing to put in the time on purpose to produce.

Results do not just come automatically. There is no worthwhile endeavour where this happens. You can, and should, build a process that churns out results on a regular basis, but this not what I mean by automatic results. There is no magic formula or magic words that make products appear. You need to go and make them happen. Prayer is not a magic incantation that makes products appear out of nowhere. If this was the case and you could simply pray yourself into having an unlimited product like money then church intercessors would be the richest people on earth. The fact that they are not should be a hint that God is not a genie in a bottle. Invest time to bring your products into existence.

OBSERVE THE MASSES, DO THE OPPOSITE

The challenge of the human race in the 21st Century is that we have become too preoccupied with what everyone else is doing or where they are going. We have in turn lost ourselves. We set standards for ourselves not based on where we personally want to go but on the barometers set by others for us. We cannot all be the same and in order to become the best of you, you have to invest in yourself. I can almost hear you say, "Well, l do not have this or I need that to start."

My question to you is, what have you done with that which you have? If you learn how to manage your resources well such as time and money, they will open doors on to another level.

When I say that I lived intentionally to produce products, I mean that I avoided the status quo like the plague. You cannot live a life that has results if you are simply living like everyone else. The general populace does not understand the benefits of investing your time to produce results. So, they are not willing to put in that deliberation. They therefore, waste time and spend it at ordinary jobs and doing ordinary things. You do not want the results they are getting so do not live like them. You cannot be following their culture and traditions.

In the United Kingdom, there is a program that exemplifies what I am talking about so well called Goggle-box. It is all about watching other people in front of their TV as they watch the shows. This is the ultimate timewasting activity - wasting time by watching someone else wasting time! I never thought we as a people could descend to these levels of folly. According to the Bureau of Labour Statistics, in the United States people wasted over 1000 hours a year watching TV on average. That is about 2.8 hours a day.

A lot of people go to church as a social activity. Make sure you are not like these people. Do not just go to some church and not have anything to show for it. The masses do this and they live lives with nullified effectiveness. They

have nothing they can point to as results. Do you want to be like them? Is this how you want to live out your time? You are not a Christian robot who just does things. When will you see that you are being manipulated and controlled by other forces outside you. Your pastor, leaders, friends at that church are doing you a disservice when they guilt you into doing things that do not empower and encourage you. Empowerment and encouragement are what you should be getting from church.

Your time is better spent investing in yourself. You must take time to learn how to live a life with God. Having real fellowship with His Spirit where He is imparting knowledge and ideas into you at all times. Have you taken time to find peace with God? It is available and it will benefit you a hundredfold. Search it out.

Do not be a lazy child of God. Nothing will be spoon fed to you. You need to dedicate your time to finding His calling and purpose for your life. I happen to have materials that are specifically about this topic and if you go to my YouTube channel you can find them under my playlists. Sitting alone in solitude and studying these video teachings will help you to discover who you are meant to be. Discovering what you could do with your life is something worth dedicating your life to. You have no problem selling time out so you can get some small semblance of compensation, but you will not find time to discover who you are. The essence of investing time in you is empowering yourself.

It is truly about adding value to yourself. This is what you must be doing with your time. Get knowledge and wisdom. These things are more precious than silver and gold. Money is not worth as much as them. Your thinking has to be different to everyone else. You need to be thinking about how you could maximise the time you have through hard work. The combination of work and time is truly explosive if you desire to have a productive life like Jesus. You need to be concentrating, searching and researching in order to get better.

USE YOUR SKILLS TO PRODUCE

The goal is to be producing something of value, to produce something through your skills. What skills and talents have you picked up in life? Through your schooling, your studying and your self-educating. These can be used to produce products. You also have your profession. In a job, this profession is being exploited by your slave master which is your boss. They are taking full advantage of this profession all because you want to be taken care of. You are so much better than this. You have accumulated knowledge throughout your life. This knowledge is a bank vault of riches that is waiting for you to convert into something tangible for the world. There are things that you have already. You do not need to go far to see that you have been given gifts and opportunities that are honestly precious and useful. Do not complain about what you do not have that others who seems to be successful have.

The only thing is that you must make sure you are intentionally bringing out results using your given gifts. If you are a doctor and you have writing skills then where are the medical journals that should be coming out of you? The world is waiting for your healing remedies. You may have negotiating skills that you have used in business for your employer. Where is the law firm that specialises in mergers and acquisitions that is sitting inside your mind? It is a product that is waiting to be made solid. Go and intentionally find an old war horse of a law partner and find out from them what it takes to own your own firm. Perhaps as a truck driver you have not had an opportunity to share all the tremendous amount of word you have accumulated inside you. Instead of waiting for someone to notice you, why do you not start by creating a devotional for truck drivers in the form of what you yourself currently use? Encouragements on what to do when drivers are lonely and how to maximise the short time they have with their families, for example.

Beth Moore, one of the foremost authors, evangelists and bible teachers in the United States, got her start in a similarly unassuming way. Aged 18, she knew her purpose in life was to teach the bible but quickly she realized she did not know enough about the book to make a real impact. She hence set out to get more acquainted with the texts she would be teaching and find the deeper meaning of the stories.

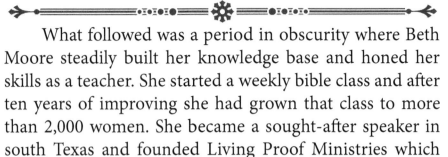

What followed was a period in obscurity where Beth Moore steadily built her knowledge base and honed her skills as a teacher. She started a weekly bible class and after ten years of improving she had grown that class to more than 2,000 women. She became a sought-after speaker in south Texas and founded Living Proof Ministries which turned her teachings into books, study courses and events. By honing her skills, Beth Moore has turned herself into a powerhouse of the evangelical Christian sphere.

We must teach our citizens to use their skills to produce remarkable products like Beth Moore does. Books, videos, audio recordings as well as projects, contracts and proposals can come from our people when we teach them this.

Do not follow pedantic religious traditions. Your new life that produces real products is not just about doing things because you are religious. That becomes a bland life and a faith that has no power to help people. It is the kind of faith that people react against because it is a counterfeit. People flocked to Jesus because His life was alive and full of results. They must be attracted to the amount of life in you too. Your Christian life is supposed to be about your personal relationship with Jesus. Do you know Him really? Has He given you your life mission? Instead of following the traditions of some religious organisation or church you should concentrate on how He speaks to you. If what your pastor is telling you does not have that life of Jesus all over it and is not making a better converter of time, then you are better off out of that church.

What Do You Do With Your Time? Do you go after a real relationsghip with Jesus? This is what Christianity is all about. It is about you and Him alone. No one else. You and Him in private with you finding out more and more about Him while in His presence. As you are doing this, He is showing you more about yourself and how you can be more like Him. This is a beautiful Christian relationship with God. It is not you and a church. Please do not get me wrong here. I am not against church. I actually run a church. I am a pastor of a church. I am just here to point you to your Saviour and not to an organisation of people.

In conclusion, this chapter was a completion of my own story of conversion. I took my productivity to a higher level by looking at the potential I had and resolving not to be like everyone else. In the next chapter, I will show you how little time we have and that we are racing against the clock.

THE GOLDEN NUGGETS

1. To get better at converting my time into products, I had to go through a massive seeking and learning process with God.

2. With consistency and patience, the results I intended started coming out.

3. I could not do this if I lived like everyone else. Traditions and culture could not be the driving force around me if I wanted to be a producer of products.

4. You need to produce products through your skills and your knowledge, the things that you have.

CHAPTER 14
A RACE AGAINST TIME

CHAPTER 14
A RACE AGAINST TIME

In the last chapter, I concluded thoughts on how to convert the time you have. Now I will show you how important it is to live life with a sense of urgency. After all, we are all in a race against time.

THE DISAPPEARING LIFE

We didn't lose the game; we just ran out of time.

Vince Lombardi,
5-time Superbowl winning coach

In earlier chapters, we have spoken about what you need to be doing with your time. This is through converting it into value that you can add to yourself and to others and also converting it into products. Now I would like to emphasize how you must act with urgency. Vince Lombardi was very realistic about the finite nature of time in an American football game. Time is also a finite resource in your life. In the same way that you lose when the clock has run out with your team behind, so will you have lost if your life ran out and you had not produced value.

Whether you like it or not your life is disappearing. It is slipping away with every passing second. You may view the disappearing that is taking place as an hour here and a day there, but this is how it vanishes. Those days that you are comfortably going to a job or attending non-stop church events, they represent what time is getting away from your grasp.

THERE IS A RACE YOU MUST RUN

Without knowing it, you are in a race. This is a metaphor. You are in a race to make sure your life is being invested. You have to consider that the race started when you were born but from then until you started applying the principles in this book, you have been absent minded at the start line. Finally, God has grabbed your attention and is motioning you to start running. You have to invest the time you have no matter how late in the race it now is.

There are no more excuses. The race you are in is a race against time. A race against time to make best use of time. Time is frantically counting down on the clock of your life. It demands that you take what is left of it by the scruff of the neck and get busy investing it into something tangible that you can show. You do not know the day that your time runs out so your urgency of action has to reflect how seriously you take this mandate from heaven.

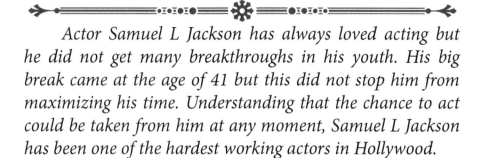

Actor Samuel L Jackson has always loved acting but he did not get many breakthroughs in his youth. His big break came at the age of 41 but this did not stop him from maximizing his time. Understanding that the chance to act could be taken from him at any moment, Samuel L Jackson has been one of the hardest working actors in Hollywood.

Where most A-list actors make one big movie a year, Sam Jackson has been consistently making between three and four a year for the last 20 years. This has helped him to catch up to and overtake those who started their acting careers before him. The body of work that Samuel L Jackson has produced is impressive by any standard and you would never guess that he was a late bloomer.

Samuel L Jackson is definitely someone who is running his race as someone with purpose. You would think that as a multi-millionaire already, he would not need to be working so hard racing against time. For you, I am sure that you have not yet achieved as much as Samuel L. Jackson. So why are you not urgently competing to produce something with your fast disappearing life?! You too, no matter where you are on the spectrum of life, can take charge of the days of your life.

It is so important to see yourself as running this race against diminishing time. Too many of us are living a spaced-out life staring into an abyss. We are watching the distractions that so easily take us astray. If you have ever walked a dog, you will know how distracted they can get.

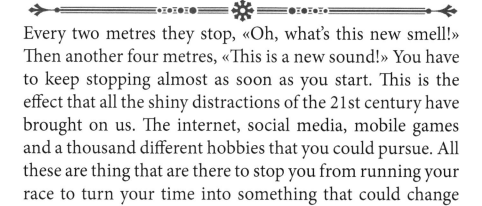

Every two metres they stop, «Oh, what's this new smell!» Then another four metres, «This is a new sound!» You have to keep stopping almost as soon as you start. This is the effect that all the shiny distractions of the 21st century have brought on us. The internet, social media, mobile games and a thousand different hobbies that you could pursue. All these are thing that are there to stop you from running your race to turn your time into something that could change the world.

You have no excuse that you can use to get out of your race. Whether you realise it or not, you are running out of time and so you are racing against it. Unfortunately, when it is time to die, you are not asked whether you were ready or not. This is the source of a lot of pain people have when they are diagnosed with a terminal disease. Many times, they are not ready to go because they counted on being able to do the things they really wanted to later on in their lives. Things like cultivating a better relationship with our children, having a dream travelling experience or doing something for God. These are the things you have to be spending your time on right now not later. If you want to travel to Israel for an experience of the spiritual holy land of your faith, why do you not do it now and add the value of the visit to yourself?

«As long as it is day, we must do the works of him who sent Me. Night is coming, when no one can work.»

Jesus of Nazareth, John 9:4

In chapter 12 of this book, I shared how Jesus was effective in His three and a half years of work. This statement above goes a long way in explaining His urgency and productivity. There was a gentle pressure He felt over Him to get on and do what He knew He was called do. Jesus knew there would come a time afterwards when the work could not be done anymore no matter how much He desired it to be done.

He likens that time as night time. If day time was the only time He could get things done, then night time would be inevitable close of that time. Daytime comes for a certain number of hours. The sun is shining brightly in the sky and at times it may seem as if it will never go down. However, if you notice carefully enough you will see that the position of the sun is changing slowly in the sky as each hour goes by. So, it is with life. You know that the energy you had in your teens is different to what you have in your thirties and forties. It is a sign that the night time of life hastens.

THERE IS NO TIME TO WASTE

What do you need to be doing with the daylight hours of your life? Instead of wasting or spending this time, you have a race to run. Your race is to make sure time is converted into something. Time has to be invested in you so that you can invest it later into others and into creating products.

There is not a breath to be wasted. Every second, every minute, every hour and ultimately every day that is passing, your race is to make sure it is converted. It all adds up you see. The days add up slowly to become weeks. Then before you know it the weeks have turned into months. The amount of people who marvel when the New Year comes. They usually swear that it felt a shorter amount of time had passed in the year than the previous one. Now we know scientifically that this is just an illusion because the time is the same, but you must understand what people mean. It is a sign that the year has been spent doing mundane tasks so much so that the days and seasons just become blurred into one. Convert the year instead. Break down each component of that block of time and turn it into valuable products.

You are in a race against time and you have many enemy who does not want you to win. The enemy is not necessarily concerned with whether you complete the race or not, it is more about what you do that scares him. If you get the whistle blown on you while you are distracted in the bushes just off the race course, it would be a much more desirable result for your enemy.

In your race, there are other runners like your family, your spouse, your children and so on. There are not only other people but there are obstacles that come into your path and things that take your attention that have nothing whatsoever to do with your race. The skilful runner will recognise that he or she is running a race that is their own. So even though we help others run and some sections we

do alongside our loved ones, we are still responsible for our own time. You cannot use the excuse, "I could not convert my time because of my wife."

THE FIGHT FOR YOUR LIFE

With all that is there to trap us, we must realise that this race is in fact a fight. You have to fight all the different things that are thrown against you to prevent you from using your time wisely. It is totally understandable when you have debt in your life, for example. It is difficult to do anything with your time than work when you have creditors hanging a guillotine over your neck. However, understand that this was the reason debt was brought into your life in the first place: to get you out of investing and converting your time. The system wants you stuck working forever. You have to wage a war and fight against the system.

It is up to you to ensure that no hour in your life is wasted. I challenge you to go ahead and do this on a daily basis. Ensure you are walking aware of what you are doing all the time. When things rear their ugly heads, and try to stop you from converting time so you can waste it on them instead, you now have the ammunition to stop yourself from going down that route.

The best runners are not swayed in this way. They are using their time either as an investment in themselves, an investment in value added to others or an investment in a product that must change the world or expand the Kingdom of God.

Consider the life of Sir Ken Robinson, the renowned British educationalist. At age four, he unfortunately contracted polio and permanently had the limp to show for it. He could have seen this as a reason to spend his days in complaining and having a victim mentality but Ken chose a different path. He doubled down on his studies and after a scholarship, went from a working-class home to a grammar school in Liverpool.

While he was studying English and drama at university Ken Robinson's mentor introduced him to culture and he learnt how to explore his own mind as well as that of his students. Sir Ken Robinson went on to influence education by raising awareness for the arts in a schooling culture that only glorify mathematics and sciences. He has advised the United Kingdom government on education and been on many boards to increase the profile of the arts.

His book, The Element, is a great analysis on how knowing what you are good at and what you love can be the key to a happy and successful career. Ken keeps on running his race giving speeches, travelling around the world and raising his family because he will not look at his seeming disability.

You too can be like Sir Ken Robinson if you do not let hurdles stop you from running. Polio could not stop him. Being poor and working class could not stop him. What is stopping you in your own life that you need to fight today? Wrestle your time and your life from these things. Fight like a man!

What are the results of your running? They must be tangible and visible to other people. Tudor Bismark, the Zimbabwean church father, once defined patience as not only waiting without activity - patience is persistent activity! Many Christians try to disguise their lack of action and results as patience or waiting on the Lord.

When you see as I have shown that you are in a race against time, What Do You Do With Your Time? The essence of this question is getting you the reader to make sure that your time is not just disappearing into thin air. In your thoughts, there must be the constant and gentle reminder of a ticking clock at all times that makes you wake up from your stupor and start doing something, producing something.

It is not acceptable for your life to simply disappear into some abstract mirage. As if you are on a crazy, drug-induced trip. God requires much more accountability from you. You cannot be like everyone else in this generation. Our generation has been taking the immature behaviour of children and passing it as acceptable for adults. We are not teenagers wandering around on drugs and unable to account for their behaviour. You are called to a higher standard than this. You are in a race against your disappearing life. Run well.

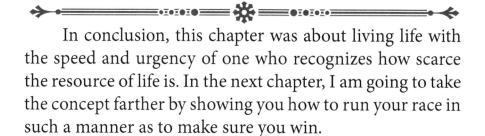

In conclusion, this chapter was about living life with the speed and urgency of one who recognizes how scarce the resource of life is. In the next chapter, I am going to take the concept farther by showing you how to run your race in such a manner as to make sure you win.

THE GOLDEN NUGGETS

1. Whether you like it or not, your life is disappearing.

2. You are in a race to make sure that it is being invested before it runs out.

3. You have to fight to make sure that time is converted before your life is over.

4. What you are trying to do is to ensure that no hour is wasted. It needs to be invested in you, other people or producing products.

CHAPTER 15
RUNNING YOUR RACE TO WIN: HOW I CONVERT NOW

CHAPTER 15
RUNNING YOUR RACE TO WIN: HOW I CONVERT NOW

Last chapter we introduced the metaphor where you look at your life as a race in which you are racing against your time and now, I would like to show you a picture of what it looks like to be winning in that race!

WHAT WINNING LOOKS LIKE

We said, in the last chapter, that you have to be aggressive about winning the race against time. What does that look like? You only win when you succeed in converting all those seconds, minutes and hours into a product, that is to say, when you have something to show for that time. A win comes in the form of an investment that you make into your destiny to make yourself big enough on the inside to be productive.

Are you investing in you? Richard Branson is a multibillionaire today at the helm of the Virgin group but you do not understand the investment in time that he made in his teens and twenties to get there. You see him now after he has won his race and is enjoying the benefits. You do not see the days he was hitchhiking to Europe with CDs that he was selling as he learned the ropes of being a merchant.

If you want to win your own race against time then invest into your own land which is your field of expertise.

You need to get to that place where you show value. Are you able to succeed in showing value in other people's lives? Are there any people who can say you have deposited good things into their lives? Are their lives better off because you took time with them? In a demonstrable way do you affect anyone's life? That is being of value.

The place where it starts is if you add demonstrable value in your own life. It is impossible to impart someone else if you yourself are running on empty. It is taxing on you when you give value to others so ensure you are not empty. For me to add value to my Facebook live video listeners on a twice daily basis for a large period of 2016, I understood that I needed to spend time investing in myself otherwise I would not have anything worthwhile to give.

IT'S UP TO YOU

For me, the story that I started to give you about how I convert into products has a happy ending. The realization of the truth came at the time that I started to produce four products in a year. I was measuring products on a quarterly basis. This was a good regularity for me considering I had started just producing one a year. When I got to producing four products a year it made things simple for me in my mind. I started to realise something that I had not thought

possible before and it made me happy. It occurred to me that my productivity was up to no one else but me.

I realised that I, and no one else, decide how much product I can produce. Whether it was one product a year, four, ten or perhaps even twenty I had the choice. The power to achieve this was inside me. God had already placed the ability there and I just had not managed to see it yet. What I do with my time was solely up to me, so I could make excuses or I could produce products. The truth of the matter is that there was no limit on me.

In an interesting movie called Limitless, starring Bradley Cooper, there was a thought-provoking premise that I would like you to consider. The producers tried to explore the limitless bounds of the human brain and they made it into a superpower of some sort to be able to access and use a larger portion of our brains. The reality, however, is closer to home than we think. We can be as productive as Jesus if we just allocate our time right for it. The limit I had put on myself that initially got me producing only one or two products a year had only been artificial. It was only fear that had prevented me from taking action but now I had cracked the secret. Have you put a limiter on your mind and brain power?

Where was this secret? I realised that I decide my discipline. Discipline is a misunderstood and thus maligned word that has been forgotten these days. In a rather spoiled generation, it seems the negative connotations of the word

discipline are making people shy away from it. Discipline is training oneself to do something in a controlled and habitual way.

> *"Discipline is the bridge between goals and accomplishment."*

> Jim Rohn,
> Author and motivational speaker

What the author above spoke about is exactly what I did. I disciplined myself in order to chart a path between my goals and reality. I trained myself to convert time into multiple products in a controlled and habitual way. Through my deliberate decisions, I set aside time to study how to do it and equipped myself with the training to produce my products and the results were as predictable and sure as anything.

TRAIN YOURSELF

When the apostle and early church father Paul of Tarsus spoke of running a race, he said,

> *«Do you not know that those who run in a race all run, but one receives the prize? Run in such a way that you may obtain it.»*

> 1 Corinthians 9:24

To obtain a prize in a race you have to win. That takes as much training as you want to win the race. Those who really want to win will take a lot of time to be disciplined.

I had to cut out the distractions that life put in front of me. Again, I had to be the one who decided how much distractions I could cut out of my life. There were both good and bad distractions around me. Remember that at the time I was getting better at converting products I was the pastor of a rapidly growing church. There were needs that arose in this area which were not necessarily bad problems but I realised I could not do everything so I got other people to deal with those things. Yes, there were also the run-of-the-mill distractions that try to get everyone of us off course which I needed to cut out. What do these distractions look like for you? Do you spend a lot of time dealing with them? What Do You Do With Your Time?

The question becomes how much can I cut out frivolity around me? Frivolous things are the small things that seem inconsequential. The things you can almost laugh about. Fun little things that take a minute here and a few seconds there. These may seem like no time lost at first, but the resultant effect on your day after you add all these things is something to truly consider. The fact is that frivolity wastes your time.

Lenny is a typical young man embroiled in a frivolous life in New York city. He spends every waking moment of his life trying to attract and sleep with as many women as

possible. The clothes that Lenny buys, the places he visits and the car he drives are all motivated by his libido. Without a true purpose, he has defined his manhood in a way that can be only described as silly.

The many hours (and dollars) Lenny spends in nightclubs, at parties and on dates could be better used in building his life if only he knew how to get out of the cycle of frivolity he has been caught in. He could be investing that time in finding out what it means to be a man, how to use that natural charm he has and building a solid future for himself.

Perhaps you may be judging Lenny, but do you have frivolity that takes up your own time? It may not be sexual escapades but what is it for you? It is taking up your time as well and you need to free yourself so you can run your race better. Many young men in today's society are like Lenny to a large extent, defining their manhood by the number of notches on their bedposts. What if more of that natural energy was turned to productivity on a huge scale. We can teach them that they can run the race of their life in a better direction. We would have less unwanted pregnancies, fewer fatherless children, fewer disillusioned and damaged women.

As for me, I realised that I decide how much I let my friends spend time with me. I used to be a people guy wanting to make people happy. I am naturally a social person and people are attracted to that. If I was not careful, this pressure to be social could have turned into a trap for my time. Culturally some people expect you to be with them all the time and be discussing matters that amount to nothing or even gossip. You do not have time for that. In the Nigerian community living in Europe, there is an expectation that people have to visit other Nigerians and spend lots of time with them. I had to decide to nip this in the bud as someone who comes from here. I love my friends and fellow countrymen. I hope you do not get me wrong here. Unfortunately, the amount of time that I let them spend with me could make or break what I want to achieve in producing value products.

In the past I used to spend time with people just for the sake of it. The people were around me and it was simply expected that we take time to visit with each other. There was no purpose to all this time spent however. If asked what the result was I would struggle to find one. The behaviour was so ingrained in me and the people around me that we never questioned ourselves. We did not consider our different callings in life when we were together we just socialised. You must think in situations where you have family or friends that are demanding your time that you cannot let people who are not running your race influence how you run. It is your race and you are the one who will be asked to account for your time.

The only exception that I allow is when you are adding value to people. Consider the time that I spend doing my Facebook live videos. It is another thing totally

if you are purposefully spending time like I am doing with my Facebook followers on a daily basis. I record videos on a regular basis which works out at about 4-10 hours a week and this add ups over the months and the sustained amount of time that I am doing it. All this time invested is compounding to create results that are multiplying me and expanding the Kingdom of God.

I am careful about what is happening when I speak with people now. It is not just a social exercise. When I talk to people we are purposefully taking about things that could improve them in life. I am also looking to discuss things that could improve me as well. Remember the framework that I work on when I am investing my time. I look to invest it in things that add value to me, add value to other people or to create a product. We are usually talking about things that could improve our world. Things that can benefit the world. What I mean is that we only conversate about adding value to each other and bettering ourselves. This is totally different to how I used to be.

BEWARE THIEVES OF TIME

In those old days, I would spend time with people because I wanted them to like me. I did not want them to think bad about me in any way. A lot of you are like this too with the need to be liked by everyone. Let me burst your bubble now before you waste your time. It will not happen. You will not be liked by all the people in your life. There are just some who will always think bad about you.

The bad part is that you also will not be producing results. I determined to disappoint a few people so that I could be considered by God to be winning my race against time.

You may ask, what do I practically do to rid myself of distractions? I do not carry a phone anymore. I already have quite an old mobile phone anyway which is the first step. The fascination which exists nowadays with smart phones is amazing. These devices are extremely distracting especially with all the apps that exist. I can more than afford a smartphone but I just choose not to have one. People around me and who I lead in my church, were appalled when I showed them the last phone I had, a Nokia that was over ten years old. It was sufficient for what I needed it for, so I saw no need to change it and pay more money to have more distractions around me. The newer phone I own now, I do not carry with me. I specifically have it when I need to use it, which protects my time.

Another thing that I discover was what made me decide to get rid of my phone. I found that people would just call me out of nowhere. This again is quite unhelpful especially when you are trying to produce products with your time. If you are not careful you can find yourself being carried away into conversations that snatch up your time. I find this with immigrants who live in first world countries. They are constantly on the phone with people from their home countries. Do you really need to speak with each of your siblings for a full hour on each night of the week? Is this honestly the best use of time? Or could you do better

by using those hours and minutes to invest in something that will benefit them more in the future when you add value to them? What are you doing with your time?

The television is another practical example of a time-wasting device. I got rid of my television in my house twenty years ago and that was fortunate for me. The number of people reading this book who are placated and duped out of their destiny by the television set is staggering. The television itself is a great invention God gave to mankind and it can be used in so many ways to get a message to people. You must understand, however, that there are producers and consumers for the content on television. The producers happen to be the ones who determine what the consumers consume from television and as long you are on the consumer side of the equation, you are wasting time. This is not good enough for what God has called you to do. Go away and create something that you can turn into a production for the television, if that is your purpose on earth. That is a better use of your time.

You cannot live your life for people. There is so much pressure from society and from your nation's culture to waste that time and trivialise it. Those of us who want to spend time doing things that are productive are looked at as snobbish or aloof. There may even be resentment and friends walk away from you. It is almost like a conspiracy to keep you unaware of what you could do with your time. The system does not want you to understand that the key to unlocking your destiny is hidden in your time. They do

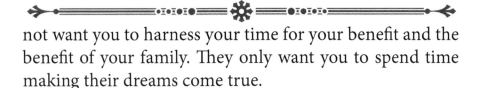
not want you to harness your time for your benefit and the benefit of your family. They only want you to spend time making their dreams come true.

Your time is being stolen from you and you do not even give it a second thought. In the movie The Matrix, the premise was mind blowing for the time it was released. Neo, Morpheus and Trinity - the protagonists - are in a system that has been created by their enemies, the machines. In order for machines to harness the immense energy that is stored in human bodies, they have to keep their minds occupied in an artificial reality called the Matrix. The system that rules our own world wants to harness the time that you have been given to enrich itself. Nobody tells you this. Your parents probably do not understand these things so they can only raise you according to the rules they were given by society. Your teachers in school will not tell you because they work for the same system. God is now giving you the chance to get wise with this material.

IT IS POSSIBLE TO GROW

I dread to think what would happen if my level of thinking about this had not increased. Imagine if I had still been measuring my life by producing only one product per year. If I had not worked on myself and grown my capacity as a human being. What would have been the result? It means between the ages of 25 and 50 I would only have 25 products to show for my life. In my estimation, that would have been failure for me. I am glad I took the time to invest in myself so I could grow into the man who can produce much more.

Life is like a casserole dish that you decide to cook. What you put inside it depends on you. You need to be intentional in order to have a successful life. Indeed, you cannot blame anyone else for what result you get out of your life. You are responsible for doing the things that you need to do to make your life the best and most productive life. This is what I am saying in this chapter and the book at large.

It is possible to grow. Imagine how you would be if you can measure your life by producing one product a day! For me I started by getting myself to a point where I could produce one product per month. I did this, as I explained in an earlier chapter, after realising I could go past having a product in a quarter. The products that I considered to be a success were having people saved, for example. I measured how many were coming into the Kingdom of heaven every month.

How many leaders were being raised in my church and the churches I raised? How many churches were being built around the world? How many organisations were being started to provide solutions to crises in my country? How many problems were being resolved by me and by the people I had raised? How many books was I writing? Personally, I considered and assessed how many books I had read as products. How many connections did I make? What was my influence level around the world? Had it increased?

What are the products that you are going to assess? For everyone it will look different depending on their own calling. What I consider a product will be different to what you look at as a product.

In concluding this chapter, there are many ways you can run your race in life, but do you have the intention to win? In the next chapter I will give you some practical tips and first steps on using your time intentionally.

THE GOLDEN NUGGETS

1. You only win in the race against time when you convert the days you have into a product.

2. After attaining four products a year, I realized that my productivity and conversion rate was solely up to me.

3. I decide how much product I produce because I decide my discipline.

4. I decide how many distractions I let into my life. My social life is controlled with my productivity in mind.

5. The time I spend with people is intentional as I know I want to impart value to them. I avoid empty conversations.

CHAPTER 16
PRACTICAL TIPS
FOR YOU

CHAPTER 16
PRACTICAL TIPS FOR YOU

In the last chapter, I showed you a picture of what living your life with a vision to win in the race of life can look like. You saw that the only factor that ultimately determines how successful you are is yourself. In this chapter I am going to share with you some practical tips you can use as you begin to use your time more efficiently.

3 VERY DIFFERENT PRODUCT PRODUCERS

Richard Branson, Joel Houston and Usain Bolt are three achievers in their own right. The products that their lives produce and that these men measure themselves are very different. Richard Branson, the founder of the Virgin Group, measures his results by the number of companies his group controls, the money it makes for its investors and the number of lives that he affects through his charitable activities.

Joel Houston, creative director of Hillsong Church, is the leader of the highly-claimed band Hillsong United. A prolific songwriter and pusher of boundaries of what church looks like, Joel measures his results based on how

many songs he writes, co-writes and how many people are reached through his work. This is very different to the perspective of a businessman.

Usain Bolt is the fastest man in the world over 100 and 200 metre sprints. His results are measured by the number of Olympic gold medals and world championships that he wins. We have stressed in the preceding chapters how much you need to produce products, with myself as the prime example but I would like to stress that there must be different things you want to measure your results with.

LEARN FROM ME, THEN DO YOU

You are not me. Your name is most probably not Sunday Adelaja and remember the words of wisdom spoken by this great inventor.

"What you are will show in what you do,"

Thomas A. Edison

The prolific inventor Thomas Edison said these words and he knew what it meant to live out your authentic identity. When we think of him, we think straight away of the many inventions he created, the company of scientists that he built and his contribution to his country.

When it comes to your own life, there must be different things that you convert into products. I do not want you feeling that because you do not write books or preach to thousands of people on a Sunday morning, you are not successful.

The things you will want to convert in your life may be different to what other people want to. There is no right way to do things so do not let anyone make you feel guilty about what you are converting your life into. Just as there are thousands of people who live in your town or village, there are also thousands of ways to win in life. You only need to find the right niche that you are created for. Like a piece of a jigsaw puzzle, there is definitely a space that only you can fill. You job is to find it.

You have to be careful that you are not swayed in your core belief. Everyone is biased. I am sorry to say that few leaders and people of authority in your life have the Godly perspective or wisdom to recognise what is right for them may not be right for you. We all see life through the tinted glasses of what we want in life. This shows itself in that most pastors see the most important type of products as relating to full time church ministry or at least products that help them build their church.

Most businesspeople feel that if someone is not making a lot of money, then they are not producing products of value. The same with educators, politicians and the list goes on. So, the person who you look to for advice, let us say

your pastor, will almost always steer you in the direction of producing products that will help her church. There is nothing inherently wrong with this, after all investing in your church is a beautiful thing that God rewards, but if God has not called you to do that then you are not investing time in the best way.

FINDING YOUR CALLING

There is a better way that you can spend your time. I highly recommend that you must find out your calling. What is calling? It is that career or vocation that strongly urges you towards itself in a way that you cannot get away from. It «calls» you because you were made for it. You must search out your gift. There are definitely some things that you have been given as tools to take life on and win. These tools are indispensable if you are going to produce the products that are stored in you. You need to look intently for your life purpose. Your reason for existing needs to be uncovered. This is by far the best way to live.

The step that follows on from finding your calling, your gift and your purpose is that you need to convert them! It is all good and fine to find them out. In fact, it is rather exhilarating to go through the process of self-discovery. There is a lot of adventure when you are getting to know yourself; what you are good at and what you are not, as well as what makes you tick. It can actually be so exciting that many are stuck in this discovery phase. You need to go on and do something about it when you have caught on to

your talents. You must convert it all in order that there may be a truly provable result of your time and what you have done with it.

How can you find out your calling, you may ask? This is a process of self-discovery that will involve getting into a quiet place with your thoughts and the God who created you. It is indeed a way you can invest in you which is something we spoke of in Chapter 3. Finding your calling counts as part of the ways you can invest your time. So, try not to be too quick to get into producing products when you have not figured out what to invest in yourself. After all, you can only produce products consistent with what is inside you and if that is not right, your results will therefore not be good. If you would like help on finding your calling then you do not have to go too far. I coincidentally have a book entitled Who Am I and a series of messages on video and audio on Finding Your Calling.

The series would be a very good place to start as I deconstructed all the parts of what it takes to find your calling and I converted it all into one hour messages. Visit my video blog **www.sundayadelajablog.com** or my YouTube channel Sunday Adelaja Official so that you can know what to focus on in your search. You will see what gifts to centre on and how to discover those gifts. There are several topics which I explore to help you in this process of uncovering your calling. These include introspection, analysis of your past and history, evaluation of your strengths and natural inclinations as well as what people who know you say about you.

I challenge you to spend real time looking at each of these areas. It will not be enough to give them a cursory glance and then move on. The minimum amount I recommend is forty hours. The reason why I say it is important to spend at least forty hours of deep study on these video or audio messages is because you spend a forty-hour working week all the time on autopilot without even thinking about it. What we are talking about here, uncovering your calling and purpose, is much more crucial than mere monetary compensation.

You have to be intentional and purposeful regarding how you convert your time. If you are investing it in the wrong area of life then it can be devastating. Among older people, one of the biggest issues they grapple with is regret. After you are 70 years old, your time has passed and if you invested it in something you should not have, you will regret it. You will ask yourself, «What did I do with my time when I had strength? When I had a full life ahead of me? When I had opportunity?» And regret is never a good thing.

POINT YOUR EFFORTS IN THE DIRECTION OF YOUR LIFE

Instead of regretting later, take time now to ask, «What is the point of my life?» What is the mission that God gave you? Everything you convert your time towards will need to point in that direction. Perhaps you know that your calling and gifting point towards you being a leader in

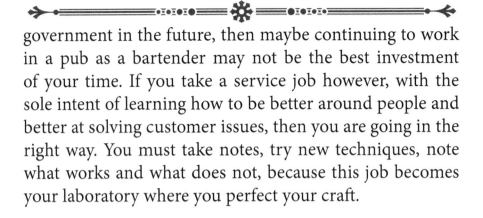

government in the future, then maybe continuing to work in a pub as a bartender may not be the best investment of your time. If you take a service job however, with the sole intent of learning how to be better around people and better at solving customer issues, then you are going in the right way. You must take notes, try new techniques, note what works and what does not, because this job becomes your laboratory where you perfect your craft.

You do not have to be like me. After all you are not me and you are not called to do exactly the same thing as me. The things I am showing you through all these examples are where I bring forth products. I totally understand that may not be where you bring forth your products. Each one of us have our own uniqueness and place in the world.

Consider again the three people I gave as an example at the beginning of the chapter, Richard Branson, Joel Houston and Usain Bolt. If Joel tried to start his own airline trying to be like Sir Richard Branson, the results could be bad in so many ways. What if he was so bad as that business that he ended up losing everything; his wife, his house, his money? What if he got so discouraged from his dismal results that he gave up on his faith? This is happening far more often than you can imagine. Usain Bolt will be far happier chasing down Justin Gatlin on the track than playing acoustic guitar for the Hillsong United band.

There are too many of us forfeiting the joy that God has put in our own vocations because we are trying to bring

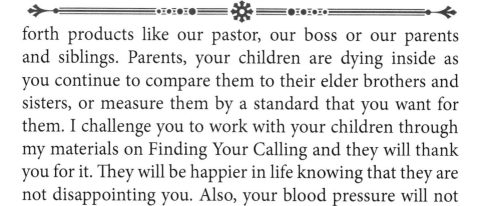

forth products like our pastor, our boss or our parents and siblings. Parents, your children are dying inside as you continue to compare them to their elder brothers and sisters, or measure them by a standard that you want for them. I challenge you to work with your children through my materials on Finding Your Calling and they will thank you for it. They will be happier in life knowing that they are not disappointing you. Also, your blood pressure will not fluctuate when you think they are failing to achieve in life.

Where is the true area you should bring forth your products? Maybe God wants you to bring forth products in medical breakthrough. Products that will lengthen the lifespan of people, increase the quality of life for the aging world population or eliminate some of the diseases that have ravaged the African continent and other developing nations. Maybe God wants you to bring forth products in scientific discovery. Global warming, decreasing water supplies and atmospheric pollution are only but a few issues that are crying out for someone to enter the laboratory with Godly wisdom and come out with answers.

Perhaps God wants you to bring forth products in the computer industry. The commercial internet is only about twenty or so years old and only starting to mature. If you think personal computing and social media are the best innovations to ever bless mankind, then you are in for a surprise. Nations like Israel and regions like Silicon Valley in California have dedicated a lot of resources into producing technology products. Could your country benefit if you did your own part?

Perhaps you are supposed to bring forth products in education. The education that our nations' children are being put through are defunct and outdated. Perhaps it is the economy for you. Countries that have relied on certain commodities to boost their economies are being shocked as things change virtually overnight. Great minds are needed to both come up with innovative products and to boost production of existing ones. Perhaps politics is your arena. We are tired of corruption, nepotism and divisive tactics instead of real leadership. Heed the call to produce that is on your life.

Do you know your calling! If you do not know it yet, then make it your top priority to find it out. It is almost pointless to look at producing products without knowing where you must be producing them. When you have your calling, you must measure it. The measuring comes in the form of having a true estimation of your capacity to produce something in your calling. You have to be honest with yourself which is why I advocate starting at a low target of how many products in a year. When you know your own strength, then make a list of what you feel God wants you to do. This is what you should be doing with your time.

In conclusion, it is important to narrow down on what you are meant to be working on with your time. You do this by finding out your calling. It is then that you can work on yourself to make yourself beneficial to the world in that particular field. In the last chapter of this book I will help you with a method of adding value to yourself.

THE GOLDEN NUGGETS

1. You do not need to be producing the same products that I do. After all we are all different.

2. Find out your own calling, gift and purpose. These are the best indication of what products you should be producing.

3. Be intentional and purposeful regarding where you convert.

4. Measure up your calling and capacity and make a list of what God wants you to do.

CHAPTER 17
MY CONVERSION METHOD

CHAPTER 17
MY CONVERSION METHOD

Last chapter I gave some practical tips on how to produce products. In this concluding chapter I will show you the results of my unique method of conversion. It has served me very well.

GETTING WISDOM

I, wisdom, dwell with prudence,
And find out knowledge and discretion.
The fear of the Lord is to hate evil;
Pride and arrogance and the evil way
And the perverse mouth I hate.
Counsel is mine, and sound wisdom;
I am understanding, I have strength.
By me kings reign, And rulers decree justice.
By me princes rule, and nobles, All the judges of the earth.
I love those who love me, And those who seek me diligently will find me.
Riches and honor are with me, Enduring riches and righteousness.
My fruit is better than gold, yes, than fine gold,
And my revenue than choice silver.

I traverse the way of righteousness,
In the midst of the paths of justice,
That I may cause those who love me to inherit wealth,
That I may fill their treasuries.

Hebrew proverb,
Proverbs 8:12-21

This poetic passage that describes how the Wisdom of God can make a man great has a beautiful truth to it. I am blessed to have seen this all come to pass in my life. The point that I have reached now is where I do not even write a book a month. Instead, I actually produce five books a month through the system that I have in place.

One product a month is not a target for me anymore. You have seen through the previous chapters that I got here through nothing complicated, I just worked on myself and grew. It took deliberate action and a certain commitment to what I knew was my calling, but you can do it too. When you have a system in place like me, you can have different parts of the production of each product as the responsibility of different members of your team. This is how products are produced by teams and organisations. In the writing of a book, there are creative writers, editors, correctors and proof readers. If coordinated well, they can become a chain that produces value and hence you can produce in a shorter time. You are not stuck doing everything but concentrating on the part you are best at doing and have time to do.

A CHAIN FOR PRODUCING PRODUCTS

The system that I have built around me now enables us to produce multiple products. I influence so many people now that I no longer produce on a monthly, weekly or daily basis. I graduated through all these levels with the passage of time so that now I produce results on an hourly basis. I evaluate each hour that I live to make sure there are some kind of products that are produced either in me or in other people through me.

Take into account our church, my international ministry and my businesses. With regards to the church, God Embassy in Ukraine, I have produced a system of assistant pastors, leaders who are multiplying my impact to the point where I can be absent doing other things while people are still being saved, healed and freed from captivity. So much so that now as I enter into the final leg of the assignment God called me for, which is returning to Nigeria and changing my motherland, I am happy to leave the leaders I have raised in charge of the work. As it pertains to my international ministry, I produce products in video messages and books that are impacting people at a level that goes beyond international borders. I also have income generating business in the form of assets and investments that I have produced.

An example of an hour I invest in producing product is the hour I was spending on Facebook every morning and every evening doing live video messages. What was

I doing with my time when I did this? I was investing in people, many of whom I did not know and had never met but I added value to them. My one hour messages were very different to anything you may have listened to before. Compare me with a lot of pastors out there. Many pastors try to make their message last an hour but they only have maybe three points that are of real value. So, they try to fill the rest of the time with fodder to make up the time.

For me this is far from the case. My messages are jam packed with points of true wisdom, applicable and practical solutions and things that I have done over the last 30 years of ministry. I do not try to sugar coat truth, I do not have inflated respect for church or cultural tradition and I speak in a way that ordinary people can understand. This makes my messages different and most of my listeners give feedback remarking how they have not heard many men like me.

I value the effect of what I am doing with these messages. The recordings were uploaded onto my blog and my YouTube channel as soon as we recorded them. I have a reason I was recording these messages and investing this time. It is not something I did just because I was bored. You must understand that I am the pastor of a megachurch with over 25,000 members. It is not for lack of things to do that I was on Facebook daily. I understand that by doing this I produce value for people in almost 100 countries. This is truly multiplying who God has made me in Ukraine to many others who can expand His Kingdom in their own

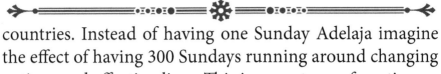

countries. Instead of having one Sunday Adelaja imagine the effect of having 300 Sundays running around changing nations and affecting lives. This is a great use of my time.

ADDING VALUE TO ME

"For my own personal growth, I had to set out on my own."

Frank Press,
2-time President of the
US National Academy of Sciences

If a man like Frank Press who advised 4 US Presidents needed to take time to grow himself, then who are you to think you can be great without adding value to yourself? This must be a challenge to you.

How do I add value to me so that I can do all the feats that I described earlier? I spend three hours a day adding value to myself in order to be effective in my endeavours. I decided a while ago that I needed to seclude myself with materials that produce wisdom for a minimum of three hours a day so that I can produce the quality and quantity of value for my listeners, my watchers and my followers. On days that I do not have as many commitments I actually spend between three and six hours investing time in myself. I realised that this is where I am most useful in order to disseminate what God has deposited in me. Take, for example, the time when I planned to create a one hour session to help people get their finances and money in order. I sat down to write an outline for one message but ended up with enough material on paper to create almost 30 one hour messages. This led to two weeks of intense teaching on financial stewardship that revolutionised the lives of so many people in Nigeria, America, the United Kingdom and Europe among others. Now ask yourself, «Where does all that knowledge, wisdom, insight and understanding come from?» I do not just wake up knowing these truths out of nowhere but I spend a lot of time placing the seed of value into me.

For those three hours, a day there are things that I do to add the value to myself. I listen to messages and read books myself on the kind of topics that make me a knowledgeable man. I am not a proud leader who despises the teachings of other men. There are people out there who know loads more about money, about time management, about work, about government and about families, than me. I invest time to learn what they have to say and add it to my own repertoire of knowledge. I spend a lot of time reading the bible, God's word, and seeing how it all relates to each other. The word is a very good place to see what is true wisdom and what is garbage. It also helps me to know what garbage is out there as well that is being taught to people as it allows me to know what deceptions I need to counter in the arguments I put forth in my teachings.

As I am separated to myself I am also doing self-education, thus adding value to myself. I research topics to see what the statistics say about marriage, poverty, African countries, churches and so on. I search the internet for videos that inform and courses that will help me.

When is the last time you educated yourself? Do you wait for your pastor to be the one to spoon feed you? He will never be able to give you everything that you need in order to produce products in your own field of calling. You must learn to feed for yourself. You are an adult. This is what you need to be doing with your time.

Consider the young man Kabelo Mokoena. He is a South African who has become frustrated with the way politics is run in his country. A devout Christian, he decided to study some political leaders in the bible and see how they managed to win the hearts of the people.

As he searched the book, Kabelo discovered the story of Absalom the son of King David who is said to have stolen the hearts of the men and the kingdom from his father. He did this quite simply by sitting at the city gate and judging the matters the citizens were bringing to the king. From this, Kabelo discovered that if you want to win people's hearts you need to solve their problems that their current leaders were not solving.

He went into isolation in order to really understand psychology as well as improve on his oratory skills as he looks to challenge the politicians who he feels prey on South Africa's poor masses but do nothing to help them. His new idea of a political party that is not ruled by an agenda or

ethnic tribalism, but is driven by what is good for the people is beginning to turn into a movement starting in his province.

This is what I have been trying to bring out in my own story that you must spend time making yourself better at the skills needed for you to achieve the dream you have. Like Kabelo, I urge you to begin working to add value to yourself.

A lot of people would not take the time to do all this, or go through all this. I know though, that by doing this I am adding products in myself. Products that most people regard are outward. I know that if there are none inside me it will only be a matter of time before there are none outside as well. The people who become burnt out and who run out of things to teach have stopped adding products in themselves. If you have not read a book since you left university you are heading down this path yourself. I understand acutely what makes me valuable. It is the wisdom inside me.

My laboratory is my mind. When I seclude myself for three hours daily, I am going into the laboratory to tinker around with ideas and concepts. I am learning how to present them and figuring out how they will be received by my listeners. Apart from this I have my books that I am writing. This is extra time that I dedicate as well. I am also raising disciples and protégés. These are people that I teach how to write books. I teach them how to teach and I show them how to become pastors. You have now had a glimpse into my personal method of converting my time.

To conclude, I have used time on a daily basis in order to fill myself up with the wisdom and content needed in order to be the kind of man who can write books, teach online and in person, disciple followers, mentor leaders and run organizations. You must also learn to fill yourself up if you want to be of value to the world around you.

THE GOLDEN NUGGETS

1. I produce five books per month through my production system.

2. I influence many people so that my products are on an hourly basis.

3. I produce value for people in almost 100 countries through my videos and books.

4. I need three hours a day to invest in myself through study, self-educating and meditating.

5. This is my laboratory where I find myself most valuable.

CONCLUSION

WHERE TO BEGIN

So, what must you do with your time? Life is short and hence your day is short too. You do not have the time that you think you do.

"If you don't think every day is a good day, just try missing one,"

Cavett Robert,
Founder of the National Speakers Association

The day you start valuing your life, is the day you start to value your time. Create a mind-shift that pushes you to excel every day because tomorrow is not promised. Always remember that the life you live today and the decisions you take, will determine the tomorrow you will have. Do not use the challenges of today as an excuse not to take action. We all have challenges, it's how we manage them that separates us. Make every day count by treating it as an opportunity to take another step towards your goal.

When you break your day down you realise that the time is limited. Even though you have a day you really have eight productive hours. If you sleep for eight hours and you spend three hours for eating, and washing, then you have family time of about five hours. So only eight hours remains as your time to be truly productive and produce products. The youth of any nation that wants to grow into an economic powerhouse must be taught this in school. If our youth grow up not believing that there is a need to be hasty with time then they are doomed to waste time as adults. It is more difficult to uproot habits like these in grown-ups than in the young. In Africa there is a saying, «There is no hurry in Africa.» This is based on a jocular view of most African countries being an hour or two ahead of Greenwich Mean Time. So, people believe that they can be an hour or two late to meetings and events. This is such a fallacy and I believe a reason for a lot of the poverty and underdevelopment of the most mineral-rich continent on earth.

My recommendation is to eke out three hours a day to produce three products in a day after you have grown your production capacity. That level is a very high calibre of activity. This means that we can start with producing a product a year then work from that. Grow into the person who can produce a product a month. The one product a day becomes reachable. It is a worthwhile dream to go for.

If you can just get to a point where you are able to produce one product a quarter you are going to be one of the most effective humans alive. This is why I say losing your job is one of the best things for you. It is actually a book I wrote as well to encourage those without a job or who are in a job that is simply stealing your time. When you have lost your job then you are not bound by that work. You can decide what you want to do with your life. You can be the one to decide what do you do with your time.

When time is in your own hands you can decide which products each of your passing days produces. You can structure your time in order to achieve that. When you are more aware you can monitor your passing life. It does not need to pass as if it was water going through your hands.

You must be in control of the passing of your life. Take charge properly and make sure that you are actually converting time into something of value. When you do this, you live a life without regret or remorse.

Measure your life by the products and results you produce. Measure your life by the value you added. If you apply it and heed what I am talking about, this topic will be revolutionary and life changing. Your own life will change. The church you are a part of will change. The economy of your country will benefit as more products are produced and traded,

Study this material over and over until it becomes part of you.

SUNDAY ADELAJA'S
BIOGRAPHY

Pastor Sunday Adelaja is the Founder and Senior Pastor of The Embassy of the Blessed Kingdom of God for All Nations Church in Kyiv, Ukraine.

Sunday Adelaja is a Nigerian-born Leader, Thinker, Philosopher, Transformation Strategist, Pastor, Author and Innovator who lives in Kiev, Ukraine.

At 19, he won a scholarship to study in the former Soviet Union. He completed his master's program in Belorussia State University with distinction in journalism.

At 33, he had built the largest evangelical church in Europe — The Embassy of the Blessed Kingdom of God for All Nations.

Sunday Adelaja is one of the few individuals in our world who has been privileged to speak in the United Nations, Israeli Parliament, Japanese Parliament and the United States Senate.

The movement he pioneered has been instrumental in reshaping lives of people in the Ukraine, Russia and about 50 other nations where he has his branches.

His congregation, which consists of ninety-nine percent white Europeans, is a cross-cultural model of the church for the 21st century.

His life mission is to advance the Kingdom of God on earth by raising a generation of history makers who will live for a cause larger, bigger and greater than themselves. Those who will live like Jesus and transform every sphere of the society in every nation as a model of the Kingdom of God on earth.

His economic empowerment program has succeeded in raising over 200 millionaires in the short period of three years.

Sunday Adelaja is the author of over 300 books, many of which are translated into several languages including Russian, English, French, Chinese, German, etc.

His work has been widely reported by world media outlets such as The Washington Post, The Wall Street Journal, New York Times, Forbes, Associated Press, Reuters, CNN, BBC, German, Dutch and French national television stations.

Pastor Sunday is happily married to his "Princess" Bose Dere-Adelaja. They are blessed with three children: Perez, Zoe and Pearl.

Bill Clinton —
42ᴺᵈ President Of The
United States (1993–2001),
Former Arcansas State
Governor

Ariel "Arik" Sharon —
Israeli Politician, Israeli
Prime Minister (2001–2006)

Benjamin Netanyahu —
Statesman Of Israel. Israeli
Prime Minister (1996–1999),
Acting Prime Minister
(From 2009)

Jean ChrEtien —
Canadian Politician,
20Th Prime Minister Of
Canada, Minister Of Justice
Of Canada, Head Of Liberan
Party Of Canada

Rudolph Giuliani —
American Political Actor,
Mayor Of New York Served
From 1994 To 2001. Actor
Of Republican Party

Colin Powell —
Is An American Statesman
And A Retired Four-Star
General In The Us Army,
65Th United States Secretary
Of State

Peter J. Daniels —
Is A Well-Known And
Respected Australian
Christian International
Business Statesman Of
Substance

Madeleine
Korbel Albright —
An American Politician And
Diplomat, 64Th United States
Secretary Of State

Kenneth Robert
Livingstone —
An English Politician,
1St Mayor Of London
(4 May 2000 – 4 May
2008), Labour Party
Representative

Sir Richard Charles Nicholas Branson — English Business Magnate, Investor And Philanthropist. He Founded The *Virgin Group,* Which Controls More Than 400 Companies

Mel Gibson — American Actor And Filmmaker

Chuck Norris — American Martial Artist, Actor, Film Producer And Screenwriter

Christopher Tucker —
American Actor
And Comedian

Bernice Albertine King —
American Minister Best
Known As The Youngest
Child Of Civil Rights Leaders
Martin Luther King Jr. And
Coretta Scott King Andrew

Andrew Young — American
Politician, Diplomat, And
Activist, 14[Th] United States
Ambassador To The United
Nations, 55[Th] Mayor Of
Atlanta

General Wesley
Kanne Clark —
4-Star General And Nato
Supreme Allied Commander

Dr. Sunday Adelaja's family:
Perez, Pearl, Zoe and Pastor Bose Adelaja

FOLLOW
SUNDAY ADELAJA
ON SOCIAL MEDIA

Subscribe And Read Pastor Sunday's Blog:
www.sundayadelajablog.com

Follow these links and listen to over 200
of Pastor Sunday`s Messages free of charge:
http://sundayadelajablog.com/content/

Follow Pastor Sunday on Twitter:
www.twitter.com/official_pastor

Join Pastor Sunday's Facebook
page to stay in touch:
www.facebook.com/
pastor.sunday.adelaja

Visit our websites for more
information about Pastor
Sunday's ministry:
http://www.godembassy.com
http://www.
pastorsunday.com
http://sundayadelaja.de

CONTACT

FOR DISTRIBUTION OR TO ORDER
BULK COPIES OF THIS BOOK,
PLEASE CONTACT US:

USA
CORNERSTONE PUBLISHING
info@thecornerstonepublishers.com
+1 (516) 547-4999
www.thecornerstonepublishers.com

AFRICA
SUNDAY ADELAJA MEDIA LTD.
E-mail: btawolana@hotmail.com
+2348187518530, +2348097721451, +2348034093699

LONDON, UK
PASTOR ABRAHAM GREAT
abrahamagreat@gmail.com
+447711399828, +441908538141

KIEV, UKRAINE
pa@godembassy.org
Mobile: +380674401958

Best Selling Books by Dr. Sunday Adelaja
Available on Amazon.com and Okadabooks.com

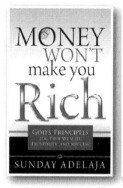
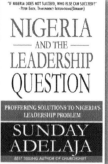
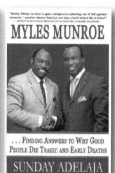
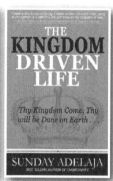

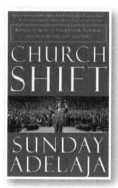
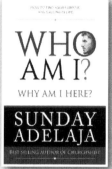

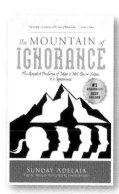

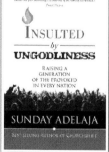
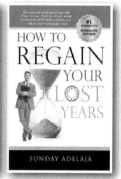

Best Selling Books by Dr. Sunday Adelaja
Available on Amazon.com and Okadabooks.com

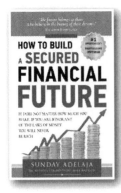 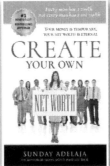 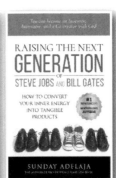 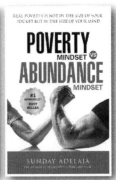

 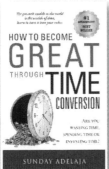 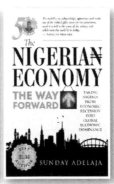 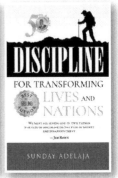

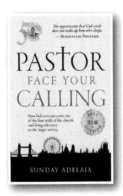

FOR DISTRIBUTION OR TO ORDER BULK COPIES OF THIS BOOKS, PLEASE CONTACT US:

USA | CORNERSTONE PUBLISHING
E-mail: info@thecornerstonepublishers.com, +1 (516) 547-4999
www.thecornerstonepublishers.com

AFRICA | SUNDAY ADELAJA MEDIA LTD.
E-mail: btawolana@hotmail.com
+2348187518530, +2348097721451, +2348034093699

LONDON, UK | PASTOR ABRAHAM GREAT
E-mail: abrahamagreat@gmail.com, +447711399828, +441908538141

KIEV, UKRAINE |
E-mail: pa@godembassy.org, Mobile: +380674401958

GOLDEN JUBILEE SERIES BOOKS
BY DR. SUNDAY ADELAJA

FOR DISTRIBUTION OR TO ORDER BULK COPIES OF THIS BOOKS, PLEASE CONTACT US:

USA | CORNERSTONE PUBLISHING
E-mail: info@thecornerstonepublishers.com, +1 (516) 547-4999
www.thecornerstonepublishers.com

AFRICA | SUNDAY ADELAJA MEDIA LTD.
E-mail: btawolana@hotmail.com
+2348187518530, +2348097721451, +2348034093699

LONDON, UK | PASTOR ABRAHAM GREAT
E-mail: abrahamagreat@gmail.com, +447711399828, +441908538141

KIEV, UKRAINE |
E-mail: pa@godembassy.org, Mobile: +380674401958

Printed in Great Britain
by Amazon